W9-CTE-007

The Soul of the Firm is a fascinating book. It reduces management and leadership of a business to understandable terms. It provides the raw material for others in leadership, and it provides a framework for those of us who lead organizations to measure our own efforts.

James R. Kackley
Managing Partner, Arthur Andersen & Co.,
S.C.

Bill Pollard is a remarkable business leader. This book shows him as tough and demanding. But also as fair, human, and idealistic. His management style is based on an unerring belief in the dignity and potential of each individual.

Lord Griffiths of Fforestfach
Goldman Sachs International Ltd.

I have admired Bill Pollard's value-based leadership. *The Soul of the Firm* reinforces this strong message.

Phillip B. Rooney
President and COO, WMX Technologies

The direct relationship between developing people and growing profitably comes crystal clear in this book as in no other. What a story! It's both a fifty percent return on equity *and* changed lives.

Bob Buford
Buford Television Inc.

This is a "must read" for anyone who questions whether following biblical teachings can help a company become successful. What William Pollard has done at ServiceMaster is not only a model for any successful company, but a model of how managing by your values is a foolproof strategy.

Ken Blanchard
Co-author, *The One Minute Manager*

~ THE SOUL ~
OF THE FIRM

C. William Pollard

Chairman of the ServiceMaster Company

HarperBusiness
A Division of HarperCollinsPublishers

ZondervanPublishingHouse
Grand Rapids, Michigan

A Division of HarperCollinsPublishers

The Soul of the Firm
Copyright ©1996 The ServiceMaster Foundation

Co-published by HarperBusiness and ZondervanPublishingHouse, divisions of HarperCollins*Publishers*.

Requests for information should be addressed to:
  Claire E. Buchan
  The ServiceMaster Company
  One ServiceMaster Way
  Downers Grove, Illinois 60515

Library of Congress Cataloging-in-Publication-Data

Pollard, C. William.
        The soul of the firm / C. William Pollard.
            p.   cm.
        ISBN 0-310-20103-9
        1. Management—Biblical teaching.   2. Business—Religious aspects—Christianity.   3. ServiceMaster Company—Management—Case Studies.   I. Title.
    HD38.P625   1996
    658—dc20   96-33835
                                                                                                              CIP

International Trade Paper Edition 0-310-21051-8

Interior design by Sherri L. Hoffman

Printed in the United States of America

96 97 98 99 00 01 02❖ DH/ 10 9 8 7 6 5 4 3 2 1

This edition printed on acid-free paper and meets the American National Standards Institute Z39.48 standard.

Dedicated to the people of ServiceMaster,
who make it happen every day.

CONTENTS

FOREWORD

In the fall of 1986 the principal owner of Terminix International, E. W. (Ned) Cook, decided to sell the company. As president and chief operating officer of Terminix, I was assigned the task of presenting the company to all potential buyers. That is when I first met Bill Pollard. He was then the president and chief executive officer of ServiceMaster Industries Inc., one of several companies interested in acquiring Terminix. I recall it as a pleasant introduction. After my pitch about how great an organization Terminix was and about its excellent potential for growth, Bill asked to meet privately with me. I expected to further discuss the financial and market projections I had presented, much as I had done with other interested parties.

Imagine my surprise when, instead, we embarked on a conversation about people and our respective philosophies of management, leadership, and responsibility to our associates in the workplace. I found it unusual but refreshing to talk about value, the dignity and worth of the individual, the significance of God in the work and lives of people, and the essence of the four objectives of ServiceMaster that form the basis of the firm's corporate culture. I could certainly relate to these expressions of value and responsibility, since they clearly reconcile with my personal perspective on people and ethical standards. But interjecting these thoughts into a discussion relating to a potential business acquisition was, to say the least, unexpected.

I must say, however, that at no time during the course of our conversation did I sense Bill's tone or message to be threatening or confrontational. Quite to the contrary, it was unmistakably a message of inclusiveness and an invitation to share. It was a clear reflection of the philosophy of ServiceMaster: one of respect for the culture, dignity, and beliefs of all people. In retrospect, Bill was even then describing *The Soul of the Firm*.

As the negotiations continued on the Terminix acquisition, I saw other aspects of Bill's character that have been reinforced through the growth of our relationship. He was—and still is—a tough, no-nonsense leader who clearly understands his parameters and objectives and will stand his ground when the situation demands it. Perhaps a better description of Bill, the businessperson, was provided by his eldest son, Chip, when he described his dad as "a relentless negotiator, a perpetual generator of ideas, and an intense questioner" (see the afterword of this book). This is truly an apt commentary on a man committed to his faith, his family, his work, and the people of ServiceMaster.

The *Soul of the Firm* is about people and values. It demonstrates the difference they can make in the ultimate success of any organization, not simply because of their work ethic and commitment to success, but because of the impact that all of us can make in the lives of those we have the opportunity to associate with and serve.

The message in the book is clear. Leadership in the firm has a responsibility to the ethical, professional, and personal development of every individual in the organization. This can be accomplished only through the belief that all of us are created in the image and likeness of God, and a philosophy of understanding based on respect for the dignity and worth of every individual.

The *Soul of the Firm* is laid out in a simple, easy-to-follow format. The focus on values, people, and leadership responsibilities is reinforced with graphic examples of people at all levels in the organization who live what they believe. With characteristic educator style, Bill conveys the message that people—customers, associates, and shareholders alike—when treated with respect and dignity, will reciprocate accordingly. This book treats all of us to a wonderful array of useful ideas on the significance of corporate values, the recognition of leadership as a moral responsibility, and the many ways in which people join together to become *The Soul of the Firm*.

—Carlos H. Cantu

ACKNOWLEDGMENTS

A book like this is not possible without the help of many others. The inspiration to write the book came from my two mentors, Ken Hansen and Ken Wessner, both of whom are no longer living but who had a profound influence on me and many others in the ServiceMaster family. I am also grateful to my partner, Carlos Cantu, for his advice, support, and encouragement as he has read and reviewed several drafts of the manuscript.

Many others have contributed to my growth and development over the years. They include my college professor "Doc" Volkman; my partners and many of my clients in the practice of law; and friends and colleagues in the field of education or other areas of service, including Hudson Armerding, Billy Graham, Allan Emery, George Bennett, Max De Pree, Peter Drucker, Frances Hesselbein, Jim Heskett, Earl Sasser, Len Schlesinger, Jerry Hawthorne, Dick Lauber, Dick Gieser, and Don Soderquist.

My instructors in ServiceMaster are too many to mention; but over the years, our board of directors has represented a very special group—not just as symbols of authority, associates in a country club atmosphere, or approvers of my compensation—but as those who challenged my thinking, supported some of my wild ideas, and said no when I was going in the wrong direction. They acted as a group, but each of them has been a special friend and encourager to me.

Koji Chiba and Shigeharu Komai, leaders of Duskin—our partner in Japan, and Hassan Moharrak, the leader of Al Majal ServiceMaster in the Middle East, have been special friends and mentors as they have taught me the reality of working in different cultures.

My mother; my wife, Judy; and our children and their spouses have all contributed in a very special way to the process of writing this book. They have been patient and kind as they have read and reread my thoughts. Judy in her own special way has been both a critic and an encourager. A special thank you to my son-in-law, Chris Grant, who got me started. And thanks to Kay Bitts, my faithful secretary, who labored through the drafts but always with a smile. And last but certainly not least, a special thanks to my colleague, Dave Baseler. He has helped me each step of the way with the manuscript. He has been a servant to the task and, without him, there would be no book called *The Soul of the Firm*.

INTRODUCTION

It All Starts with the Person

WHAT DOES A lawyer have to say about the soul of the firm? Can a professor or businessman improve upon the answer? Life has provided me with all of these work experiences. But for me the experience of work without people is dull and empty. People provide the life, the vitality, the conscience, and, yes, even the soul of the firm.

ServiceMaster, the firm for which I work, has a soul. We do celebrate profits, but as Peter Drucker, the father of modern-day management, has said, we are also a firm that "has made a business of the training and developing of people." Although we spend much of our time involved with the mundane tasks of serving others, we have been described by Jim Heskett of Harvard Business School as a firm that "has broken the cycle of failure and has basically reengineered jobs, provided training to people, and attempted to deliver a level of self-esteem that many workers have never had in the past."

Is there a secret to the ServiceMaster success story? What is our culture all about? Will it work in other environments? Is it sustainable?

Twenty years ago I was like many of you who are reading this book and asking these same questions. I was on the outside looking in, wondering about the answers and about how they might apply to me and my future. It was an important time for me as I was facing a major change in both my life and my career. After having completed five years of serving as a college administrator and professor, I had planned to go back to the practice of law. But another job offer caused me to pause and consider: Should I accept a position as a partner in a major law firm, or should I join ServiceMaster, a company that over the previous five-year period had experienced rapid growth?

If I took the business opportunity, it would mean some new and uncharted waters for me. And the job offer was indeed unique—some might even say radical. The proposed title, senior vice president, indicated major management responsibilities. But the base compensation was less than what I had been earning in the practice of law five years earlier, and my first assignment would be to work with the housekeeping team at Lutheran General Hospital cleaning corridors, patient rooms, and even bathrooms and toilets. I had never heard of a company that trained its senior executives by having them do that kind of work!

I was assured by Ken Hansen, then chairman of Service-Master, and Ken Wessner, the president and chief executive officer of the company, not to worry about my initial salary. If I performed and the company performed, my incentive compensation at the end of the year, plus the opportunity to purchase stock along the way, would more than make up any difference in my perceived loss of earnings. And they explained that my first job assignment, although different, would be good for me. I would learn lessons of servant leadership. I would experience the feelings and emotions of front-line service workers and gain some empathy for people serving others. I also would learn more about my responsibility as a manager and leader and would begin to understand how my work and those with whom I worked would influence me as a husband and a father. There was only one way to find out if they were right. I had to trust the two Kens and take a leap of faith.

It didn't take long to find out. One incident that took place during the first few days of my training is still a vivid reminder to me of how others often treat and view those who serve in routine assignments. I was working in a busy corridor of the hospital. I had just set out my wet-floor signs and was about to mop the floor. People were streaming back and forth when suddenly a lady stopped and asked, "Aren't you Bill Pollard?" I responded that I was, and she identified herself as a distant relative of my wife. Then she looked at me and my mop, shook her head, and asked, "Aren't you a lawyer?" as if to say, "Can't you get a better job?" I paused, looked down at my bucket, and said, "No, I have a new job." By this time several other people had gathered around. She was now embarrassed and leaned close to me and whispered, "Is everything all right at home?"

Many other experiences during those first few months left their mark of reality, and my learning about people continues. I still spend several days each year working alongside our front-line service workers, seeking to better understand them and the customers they serve. And as you continue through this book, you will read about our "WE SERVE" day, during which every leader in ServiceMaster has the opportunity to participate in directly serving the customer. These special days of service keep us in touch with reality.

It has been almost twenty years since I joined ServiceMaster, and the time has passed quickly. The two Kens were right on! My glass has been more than half full. It has been overflowing. I now have a different title—chairman; and for ten-and-a-half years I also served as chief executive officer. We are now more than twenty times larger than when I joined ServiceMaster in 1977, and we employ and manage more than 200,000 people and serve more than five million customers in thirty countries. We are a public company listed on the New York Stock Exchange with over 50,000 shareholders, and the combined market value of our shares is now over $3 billion. We have been described as the "jewel" among the *Fortune 1000*, and "Star Number One" by the *Wall Street Journal*. We serve hospitals, schools, and homeowners, and we trade under the major brand names of Service-Master, TruGreen-ChemLawn, Terminix, Merry Maids, and American Home Shield.

At times it has seemed like running both the sprint and the marathon as we have maintained a consistent growth record with revenues and profits up every quarter during this period. But it also has been a time of significant personal development as I have grown in my understanding of others and in my love for my wife and my family. All of my children are now adults raising their own families, and they all are active shareholders of Service-Master. You see, my job is more than an assigned task or an appointed position. It has become a way of life, and my work has contributed to the process of who I am becoming.

Writing this book was harder work than I expected. Maybe the job still is not done. Maybe it is a job that can never be finished, because this book tells a dynamic story that is being retold and revised every day in the lives of people. So what you are about to read is not just another "business" book. While it contains principles of leadership, it is not just a book about how to lead. While it includes a discussion on the importance of profit, it is not just a book about how to make money. It is, rather, a book about people and their work. It is about the firm as an organization of people at work. It is about people at work who make up the soul of the firm.

If you lead others or aspire to do so, this book is about you and the pregnant potential of the people with whom you work or whom you lead.

So, if you lead others or aspire to do so, this book is about you and the pregnant potential of the people with whom you work or whom you lead. Together you have the potential to produce value—value measured in who you are becoming, value measured in what you are producing, and value measured in the worth of your combined effort. This concept may sound too idealistic for the bottom-line pressures of the marketplace, but it is proven every day in our firm.

Our economy is made up of many different firms, some small and some big. Some we call corporations, others partnerships or proprietorships—like the local barber shop, laundry, or grocery store. The firm can also be used to describe a community or charitable organization such as a hospital or a school.

Although most of my experience and the examples used in this book come from the marketplace, with its own litmus test of the bottom line, the principles discussed are people principles and thus are universal—and also, by the way, cross-cultural.

The objective of a business firm is to maximize profits. This is called the *theory of the firm,* and it provides an explanation of how decisions made by many different and independent firms collectively satisfy the wants and needs of consumers. One economist has described this "free-market process" as the equivalent of floating in a sea of market relations like lumps in buttermilk.

Most of us have never thought of our firms as lumps or of the markets we serve as mushy buttermilk. But it is a reality that markets and the needs and wants of our customers change. The firm must go with the flow if it is to float and survive. The bottom line is often the key measurement of whether the firm has kept pace with change.

But are the demands on the firm to produce profits consistent with the development of the person? In a world of downsizing, reengineering, and restructuring, where does the person fit? Can we expect the firm to grow profitably and develop its soul? At ServiceMaster the task before us is to train and motivate people to serve so that they will do a more effective job, be more productive in their work, and, yes, even be better people. This task is both a management and a leadership challenge. It is more than a job or a means to earn a living. It is, in fact, our mission.

"Money is like manure. It doesn't smell any better the more you pile it up." If we focused exclusively on profit, we would be a firm that had failed to nurture its soul.

Does this mean we are soft on profits? Hardly. Just look at the numbers. Our profit standard is simple: for every six cents we invest, we generate a dollar's worth of revenue and get back six cents in cash flow. On an incremental basis, that is a 100 percent return on investment. People *and* profit are part of our mission. Profit is how we are measured by our owners. It provides the resources to grow and develop people.

But profit for us is a means goal, not an end goal. "What does it profit a man if he gains the whole world but loses his own soul?" The accumulation of profits in the hands of a few is never justified. Marion Wade, our founder, used to remind us, "Money is like manure. It doesn't smell any better the more you pile it up." If we focused exclusively on profit, we would be a firm that had failed to nurture its soul. Eventually, I believe, firms that do this experience a loss in the direction and purpose of their people, a loss in customers, and then a loss in profits.

We make money at ServiceMaster. Our return on equity has averaged 50 percent. During the past twenty years, a share of our stock has grown in value from one dollar per share to over twenty-eight dollars per share. Our people have produced profits and created value and, as owners of the results, they have participated in the wealth that has been created. They are celebrating work, productivity, and profit.

When you walk into the lobby of our headquarters in Downers Grove, Illinois, you see on your right a curving marble wall that stretches ninety feet and stands eighteen feet tall. Carved prominently in the stone of that wall in letters nearly a foot high are four statements that constitute the objectives of our company:

> *To honor God in all we do*
> *To help people develop*
> *To pursue excellence*
> *To grow profitably*

If you were to tour the rest of the building, you would notice that nearly all the work spaces are movable. Most of the walls do not reach the ceiling. Practically everything in the building is changeable and adaptable, just like the marketplace we serve, with its changing demands and opportunities. But the marble wall conveys a permanency that does not change. The principles carved in this stone are lasting.

The first two objectives are end goals. The second two are means goals. As we seek to implement these objectives in the operation of our business, they provide us with a reference point for seeking to do that which is right and avoiding that which is wrong. We are an inclusive environment that accepts the differences among people, yet we have a common standard that provides a unity of purpose.

This does not mean that we will do everything right. We experience our share of mistakes. But because of a stated standard and reason for that standard, we cannot hide our mistakes. They are flushed out in the open for correction and, in some cases, for forgiveness. Nor is it a standard that should be used as a simplistic reason for our financial success. It cannot be applied like some mathematical formula. It does, however, provide a foundation and a reference point for action. It is a living set of principles that allows us to confront life's difficulties and failures with the assurance that the starting point never changes and provides a reason and hope above it all.

Few people find fault with our commitment to a set of principles. Quite frankly, it is the "God language" that raises eyebrows.

Few people find fault with our commitment to a set of principles. Quite frankly, it is the "God language" that raises eyebrows. "Aren't you walking on shaky ground when you try to mix God and profits?" ask the critics. "And what about employees who don't choose to believe the way you do? Aren't you forcing your beliefs on them?"

At one of our recent shareholders meetings, a shareholder, while commending us for our profit performance, made the following statement: "While I firmly support the right of an individual to his religious convictions and pursuits, I totally fail to appreciate the concept that ServiceMaster is, in fact, a vehicle for the work of God. The multiple references to this effect, in my opinion, do not belong in the annual business report. To interpret a service for profit (which is what ServiceMaster does) as the work of God is an incredible presumption. Furthermore, to make a profit is not a sin. I urge that next year's business report be confined to just that—business."

How would you answer this shareholder? What would you say in response to the question "What is there in common between God and profit?"

I believe there is a link. Profit is a means in God's world to be used and invested, not an end to be worshiped. Profit is a legitimate measurement of the value of our effort. It is an essential source of capital. It is a requirement for survival of the individual, the family unit, and any organization of society, whether it be a for-profit company or a not-for-profit organization. If you do not generate a surplus out of your annual operations, you will not generate a positive net worth. If you do not have a positive net worth, you will be operating in the red with a deficit. No organization, whether it be for-profit or not-for-profit, can survive with a continuing deficit.

God and business do mix.... For us, the common link between God and profit is people.

God and business do mix, and profit is a standard for determining the effectiveness of our combined efforts. Work and profit are here to stay. It is the leader's responsibility to manage work within the firm to produce profit. For us, the common link between God and profit is people.

But we live and work in a diverse and pluralistic society, and some people may either question the existence of God or have different definitions for God. That is why at ServiceMaster we never allow religion or the lack thereof to become a basis for exclusion or how we treat each other professionally or personally. At the same time, I believe the work environment need not be emasculated to a neutrality of no belief. A belief that God exists and is at work is not some relic of the past, or as Stephen Carter notes in *The Culture of Disbelief*, "like building model airplanes, just another hobby: something quiet, something private, something trivial—and not really a fit activity for intelligent, public-spirited adults."

Regardless of your starting point, the principle that can be embraced by all is the dignity and worth of every person—every worker.

My belief in God is based on my faith and trust in Jesus Christ. I am a Christian. My faith is personal to me and not a corporate belief, nor can it be mandated as such. The God of my faith is the God of the Bible, a personal God who has created the people with whom I work, with whom I compete, whom I sometimes dislike, and whom I also love. I believe that God has invested each one of them with dignity, worth, potential, and freedom to choose. They make up the company for whom I work, and they give meaning to my work. My daily challenge is not just to talk about my faith, but to live my faith in the way I recognize and treat others, including those who do not agree with me or my faith. In the very direct words of our founder, Marion Wade, if I don't live it, I don't believe it.

Whether or not you share my belief or the claim of God as creator, you should examine the reality of the results of Service-Master. Regardless of your starting point, the principle that can be embraced by all is the dignity and worth of every person—every worker. It becomes a living principle as the mission of the firm is understood to include the personal development and growth of that worker.

The linking of the performance of the task with the development of the person forces the firm and its leadership to keep asking what is happening to the person in the process. What are they becoming in their work? Is the task as defined, the tools as designed, and the training as provided contributing to or detracting from the work and the worker? It is a self-energizing and correcting process that is never over and is the basis for our quest for continuous improvement in how we serve.

Any work can be categorized as either drudgery or creative. A given task or job, no matter how mundane, is not determinative. The difference is to be found in the soul or spiritual side of the person doing the task. It is that part of our being that seeks a meaning for life and work. As a person sees a reason for the task that is personally satisfying and rewarding and has the confidence that the mission of the firm is in alignment with his or her own personal growth and development, a powerful force is unleashed that results in creativity, productivity, service, quality, growth, profit, and value.

The objectives of our firm are not just carved in stone on the lobby wall. You can see them working every day in the lives of our people.

As this process of doing and becoming has been subjected to the litmus test of the marketplace, I have learned (1) to value each person as an individual with unique skills and talents; (2) to recognize the benefit and reality of diversity; (3) to harness the power of a common purpose; (4) to celebrate work, productivity, and profit; (5) to encourage empowerment, ownership, and accountability; (6) to recognize that learning is a lifelong experience; (7) to demand of leadership, service by example; and (8) to accept and build on the abilities of ordinary people and expect extraordinary performance.

As these have occurred within the context of our firm, people have learned to build on individual strengths and cover individual weaknesses, like shingles on a roof. Just as the shingles on the roof of my house overlap and provide coverage and strength, so also can the shingles of people working together, with their individual gifts and talents, provide coverage and strength for the firm.

The objectives of our firm are not just carved in stone on the lobby wall. You can see them working every day in the lives of our people. We do not worship these objectives, but use and apply them so that there is evidence of a vital, living soul at work—the soul of each person joining together with others to become *The Soul of the Firm*.

CHAPTER ONE

More Than a Pair of Hands

Henry Ford was a genius when it came to automobiles and the methods of mass production, but I believe his understanding of the worker was too limited when he asked, "Why is it that I always get the whole person, when what I really want is a pair of hands?" Unfortunately, that quote describes the attitude of some top managers today. But to protect and nourish the soul of the firm, we need more than a pair of hands; we need the whole person—and whether we like it or not, that is what we always get.

"Why is it that I always get the whole person, when what I really want is a pair of hands?"

One of the downsides of the Industrial Revolution is that it fostered the idea that a person is just a "production unit." As people have been "replaced" by machines, there has been a tendency to think of them as machines. This reminds me of an experience a friend of mine had with an answering machine. When he called, the machine answered: "This is not an answering machine; it is a questioning machine. There are only two questions in life that are relevant: Who are you? and What do you want? Most people do not know the answer to these questions. Please give your answer at the sound of the tone."

Who are we and what do we want? We are not machines; we are people, with our own fingerprints of personality and potential. Only people, not machines, can respond to the unexpected and surprise the customer with extraordinary performance. Only people can serve; only people can lead; only people can innovate and create; only people can love and hate.

We are not machines; we are people, with our own fingerprints of personality and potential.

What kind of employee do you want in your company? What kind of worker do you want to serve you in your home or in your school? We know that animals can learn a conditioned response and repeat an established pattern of behavior. But people have the potential to improve upon their knowledge, to modify, to adapt, and to exercise judgment within a framework of moral values. It is not just what we are doing, but what we are *becoming* in the process that gives us our distinct value and is uniquely human.

It is not just what we are doing, but what we are *becoming* in the process that gives us our distinct value and is uniquely human.

W. Edwards Deming, in his quest for quality, reminded us that we all are born with an intrinsic motivation, self-esteem, dignity, and a curiosity to learn. Peter Drucker provides us with that simple yet profound definition of management: getting the right things done through others. The firm has the potential to bring these two principles together and to respond to that basic ethical question of the marketplace: What is happening to the person in the process? Is she developing and growing as a whole person? Or is management just a game of manipulation that will accomplish a series of tasks for a profit, with a gain going to a few at the top and with an atrophy of the soul of the person producing the results?

We need only to pick up a newspaper to be reminded that manipulation is not just a problem of the past. People are taken advantage of at work. They need legislation to protect them (maybe not all the legislation we have today, but that could be the subject of another book). And they are forced from time to time to organize and negotiate their terms of employment with management. Sometimes the problems are not as evident on the surface and appear to be covered by short-term financial gain.

> **The firm has the potential to bring these two principles together and to respond to that basic ethical question of the marketplace: What is happening to the person in the process?**

My former partner Alex Balc once gave a very thorough report on a competing company as part of our continued attempt to stay on top in our industry. He described some of the financial successes of this competitor (which were considerable) but also reviewed some of its problems with people, purpose, and direction. I will never forget his conclusion: "This is a company without a soul." Here was a case where it was forgotten that people are unique, one of a kind, and are not just the cost of doing business or the expense of a payroll.

WHAT IS VALUE? IS MONEY THE ONLY MEASUREMENT?

IN THE MARKETPLACE we have ways of measuring the value of the combined efforts of people in the firm. It all adds up, we hope, to profits. And profits add up to net worth. If we organize the firm for public ownership, we might even anticipate value being measured as a multiple of those profits. For example, as I write this book, ServiceMaster has a book value of $750 million, yet our market value is over $3 billion.

But what is the value or the worth of a person? Can we measure this value by a paycheck, a retirement benefit, an incentive payment, or even a stock option? Is it to be measured as a net cost or an added value? Things that are unique, one of a kind, grow in value. But is this true of people?

Some years ago I purchased a Hummel Christmas plate for my wife, Judy. The price was $21.95. It was the first Christmas plate produced by the famous German firm, and the store clerk assured me it would increase in value. Recently Judy and I attended an antique auction and were surprised to see a Hummel Christmas plate just like ours being sold for more than $1,000.

What was it about the plate that caused this remarkable growth in value? Its substance had not changed, and it was not more beautiful. It had not changed size. But it was in greater demand. The original mold had been broken. Now only a limited number of plates were available, with no opportunity for replacement. All of these factors had contributed to an increased value.

There is only one mold per person and no opportunity for replacement. Yet does this count for value in our normal way of thinking as we build the firm and the people within the firm? Publilius Syrus, a famous first-century Roman writer, concluded, "A thing is worth what someone will pay for it." For him, this was not just a simple truism; it was reality. He had been a slave, brought from Antioch to Rome, where he was purchased by a wealthy philanthropist who promptly set him free. Perhaps he knew the large sum of money his benefactor had paid for him. "Am I worth that much?" he might have asked. What is any human being worth? A few dollars, which is the combined value of one's chemical substance? The price of a slave? Or a special compensation package including a sign-on bonus for a star ball player or a highly skilled professional manager?

We will never be able to pay people what they are really worth, but sometimes we act like we can. We pay people wages and incentives and then make a monetary standard the only measure of their worth. But if we are to be true advocates for people, we must not limit the measurement of human worth to what people are paid. Instead, the value of individuals must also be recognized by the contribution they can or are making in the lives of others—the people they marry, they parent, they work with, they produce for, they teach, or they serve. Two commonly recognized organizational units in our society where people contribute to others are the family and the firm. While this is a book about the firm, in a healthy society, both the family and the firm should support each other.

We will never be able to pay people what they are really worth, but sometimes we act like we can.

In the firm, people have the potential to contribute in at least three ways. First, they contribute *value to customers* with the products they produce or the services they provide. Second, they contribute *value to owners*, as their combined effort is worth more than the sum of the efforts of individual participants. And third, they contribute *value to each other*, as they learn together and experience the satisfaction of accomplishment and advancement and as they develop their own self-worth.

These three principles of *people value* correspond to three of our company objectives: To pursue excellence, To grow profitably, and To help people develop. In our firm, we encourage every worker to actively participate in improving the quality of service to the customer, to participate as owners in the profits they produce, and to participate in the development of the people with whom they work. As we seek to make this triangle of people principles work, we nurture the soul of the firm.

Today our company employs and manages more than 200,000 unique people who all have different skills and talents. Our survival and future is dependent on them working together in doing things right and in doing the right thing.

Still the question remains, "How do you do it?" How do you get people to take initiative, to grow and develop, to treat the company as if it were theirs? Obviously, you have to provide a compensation package that is fair and competitive, but any firm can do that. You also have to pay attention. You listen to your employees, get to know them, find out what makes them tick, and then help them reach their goals. That is exactly what happened in the life of Bob Ware.

My partner Ken Wessner first met Bob more than twenty-five years ago during the start-up of Norfolk General Hospital, where Bob was a floor finisher. In his first interview with Bob, Ken identified Bob's potential to work with and lead others. Although some in the hospital had concluded that Bob had no talent to manage, Ken listened and heard a person who cared about others and wanted to grow as a manager. He took a risk and asked Bob to join ServiceMaster as an assistant manager. Bob performed well in this position and was soon promoted to manager of the hospital housekeeping staff. Several years later he became a regional manager and then an area manager, a division manager, and division officer, and ultimately a senior officer of a large business group of ServiceMaster.

But Bob's story does not end there. This is not just another story of an entry-level employee making the big time as a senior officer. There came a time in Bob's life when the scope of the assignment and the extensive travel schedule no longer fit who he was and who he wanted to be. Bob wanted to stay close to home and run his own business. For the firm and Bob to continue to work for each other, the firm had to be responsive to the need for change. So he was provided the opportunity to buy a ServiceMaster franchise in Fredericksburg, Virginia, and then to add a Merry Maids franchise. He has grown these businesses as a successful entrepreneur, using them to help the people who work with him to also grow. Today we can point to many people in our company whom Bob has touched, mentored, and encouraged. They have grown and developed in what they have accomplished and in who they are becoming because leadership listened, identified potential, and then acted.

Bob's business accomplishment is not all that we should admire about him. He has also grown as a person, a husband, a parent, and a contributor to the personal development of others. He found role models and leaders in the firm who invested in him as a person, not just as a unit of production. This is all part of the duplication and reproduction process that occurs when the value and worth of individuals are identified and those individuals learn the joy and excitement of investing themselves in the development of others.

This simple truth of recognizing the potential, dignity, and worth of the individual has been one of the most important factors of the success and growth of our business.

Stories could be told of many others in ServiceMaster who caught the vision that they could accomplish something extraordinary with the support and help of others, and in so doing, they fulfilled one of our founder's dreams of building a business with ordinary people—motivated, trained, and excited about accomplishing the extraordinary in service to others. This simple truth of recognizing the potential, dignity, and worth of the individual has been one of the most important factors of the success and growth of our business.

A CAREER OR A JOB?

ONE OF THE benefits of creating an environment within the firm that contributes to the development of the person is that your employees become more committed to the firm. At ServiceMaster, one way we have recognized this commitment is by erecting a "Wall of Service" outside the entrance to our headquarters in Downers Grove. Engraved on this black marble wall is the name of every person who has served twenty-five years or more. It makes no difference whether you were the president, a franchise owner, a custodian, a plant manager, or an accountant.

In front of the wall is a white marble statue that stands eleven feet high. It is a free-flowing representation of Jesus washing the feet of a disciple. This illustration from history is a great reminder for all of us that we have the potential to grow as we contribute and serve others.

Charlie Hromada's name is on that wall. Charlie became a part of the ServiceMaster family when Terminix was acquired in 1986. He grew up in the termite and pest control business, beginning his work with Terminix while still in college. Throughout his career Charlie has made significant contributions to the company and the industry. He developed the extended termite service contract and pioneered in the design and marketing of the damage repair guarantee. When Terminix began offering general pest control, Charlie wrote the manuals, training programs, and marketing materials. He took the initiative to meet personally with Terminix franchisees to help them with training, technical, and regulatory issues in this new area of their business.

When ServiceMaster acquired Terminix, Charlie saw even more opportunity. He was willing to "bet the egg money" and, along with other key leaders, took on the personal risk of acquiring an equity interest in the future of the firm as part of the commitment to help ServiceMaster continue its growth.

What makes a person spend more than forty years thinking about how to kill bugs—all with the same company? Charlie has seen momentous changes in the firm of his initial employment. Why didn't he accept one of the many offers that came from other competitors? Why didn't he leave when E. L. Bruce sold Terminix to Cook Industries, or when Cook Industries sold the company to ServiceMaster? And why is he still working today, when he could have retired comfortably after his stock earnout provision was vested?

The answer lies partly in Charlie's commitment to the people of the firm. He says, "The commitment to a company and its people is almost like the marriage commitment. Actually, you might say I married into Terminix. When I first came with the company, I went through initial training with the manager of the Memphis office. Since I was new in town, he invited me home to Sunday dinner. It turned out he had a beautiful daughter whom I promptly fell in love with. Frankie and I got married a year later while she was still in high school. In fact, I signed her report card in her senior year. So I was committed to Frankie and to the firm. And those commitments have only grown stronger throughout the past forty years."

People are playing different instruments with different parts, but when they perform together from the same musical score, they produce beautiful music. They produce value.

But Charlie knows that commitment works both ways. Along with the commitment of the individual to the firm, there also must be the commitment of the firm to the individual—a commitment that continues to provide opportunity, understanding, and growth. Charlie says that his commitment and faithfulness to the firm have grown because the firm, through all of its changes, has continued to provide the environment in which *he* could grow. "I was always given broad areas of responsibility in which to serve and was recognized and rewarded for my work," he explains. "I think I helped to interpret the route of the firm's success. And people in the firm always thought something of me as a unique person. They cared about who I was becoming and didn't just focus on what I did."

Charlie Hromada is part of the grand orchestra of Service-Master that keeps producing a symphony of results. People are playing different instruments with different parts, but when they perform together from the same musical score, they produce beautiful music. They produce value. They are in the process of discovering who they are and what they want to be.

CHAPTER TWO

Do Not Back Away from the "D" Word

WHAT DID THE mix of people in your firm look like thirty years ago? Probably a lot different than it does today. The other day I picked up our office directory to find a phone number. As I looked through the list, I read names like Assad, Chang, Cucinella, Duzansky, Dziejma, Gonzales, Gupta, Imberri-Dattel, McGuffey, Ohbayashi, Schmidt, Smith, Swierzynski, Vanderploeg, and Zalik. Our last names often reflect our national, ethnic, or religious heritage. But what's in a name?

Diversity without unity makes about as much sense as dishing up flour, sugar, water, eggs, shortening, and baking powder on a plate and calling it a cake.

Although we often introduce ourselves and who we are by repeating our name ("Hello, I'm Bill Pollard"), is that really who we are? Is my diversity to be measured by the color of my skin, or the origin of my birth? Or is there something more? As I learn to be an advocate for diversity and seek to understand the differences and contributions of race, gender, and national origin, I am also learning to appreciate who people are, how they think, and what their gifts and talents are. In doing so, I am seeking to support what we all have in common. Diversity without unity makes about as much sense as dishing up flour, sugar, water, eggs, shortening, and baking powder on a plate and calling it a cake. All the ingredients may be there, but no one is quite sure what to do with them.

Roosevelt Thomas Jr. reminded us in *Beyond Race and Gender* of the importance of recognizing that the challenge of diversity is one of acceptance, not assimilation. But mere acceptance of differences within the firm will not accomplish results and may cause confusion, disunity, and lack of direction. It is the acceptance of difference with a commitment to a common purpose and mission that allows for both homogeneity and heterogeneity. The firm then can harness the energy and creativity of difference to produce results.

When the banner of diversity is waved for group power or retribution or for an ideology built around ethnicity, gender, or any other specific difference, the firm no longer works. It simply becomes another political tool for assertion of group rights over individual performance and contribution. This results in disunity and, in my judgment, will eventually demean the dignity and worth of the person.

One of our principles of leadership at ServiceMaster is that we pay based on performance and promote based on potential. When we use other criteria, whether it be family, friendship, race, gender, tenure, or religious faith, we take something away from the person and add a potential liability to the performance of the group. We may think we have achieved the "right" balance or mix of diversity of appearance, but the litmus test of the market is performance, not appearance or classification. Norm Goldenberg, our vice president for government affairs, puts it this way: "If you pay based on a bias, the company is doomed. And the time it takes for it to die is proportional to the extent by which you violate the principle of paying for performance."

Someone who is well aware of this principle is Clay Spitz. Clay grew up in the pest control industry. His father owned a large operation in Texas, and after college Clay entered the family business. He demonstrated talent and potential by successfully running several branches, then moved quickly to full responsibility for operations, and soon became president of the $4 million company. He recalls being harder on himself because he was part of the family, and says, "I always went out of my way to make sure that when I got promoted it wasn't because I had the right last name."

There were others involved, however, who didn't do as well. Clay remembers when his father convinced a young family member to leave public accounting and start a new branch in another city—a job for which he wasn't prepared. Eventually the person had to be removed from the position, and the branch was sold. As Clay recalls, "It was a very difficult couple of years. Had we put the right person in that job who was better prepared, it would have been different. But because it was a family member in the position, we found it very hard to make changes. We probably stuck with the situation longer than we should have, which hurt the person and cost the company a lot of money." Clay and his father eventually sold their business, and Clay became an important part of our Terminix team.

When people are recognized for performance, the integrity of the process will add to their dignity and self-worth.

When people are recognized for performance, the integrity of the process will add to their dignity and self-worth. When we patronize to "look right," we demean and take away from the uniqueness and potential of that person. In seeking to do a *good* thing, we don't do the *right* thing.

We should not, however, ignore the injustices of the past and their influence on the present. Lines of advantage and disadvantage have been drawn on a basis other than potential and performance. To be an advocate of diversity in your firm, you must seek and take the risks to provide opportunity based on potential.

And you must tear down the walls and vestiges of bias and celebrate difference within the context of performance and contribution. That leads to unity—not division.

I like the way Max De Pree, former chairman and CEO of Herman Miller, Inc., identifies diversity as an element of human worth. Referring to a firm's employees, he concludes that leaders are dealing with "God's mix." They are "people made in God's image," he says, "a compelling mystery, but unavoidably diverse."

At ServiceMaster the reference point for diversity begins with our first two objectives—To honor God in all we do, and To help people develop. This starting point becomes the basis of a social contract among the members of our firm and distinguishes it from a business where the social contract is limited to earning a profit. We are seeking to build a firm that begins with God and accepts and develops the different people He created. In the words of my friend and partner Carlos Cantu, who is now the fifth chief executive officer of ServiceMaster, "Our challenge is to enable each person in a diverse work force to perform to his or her maximum potential and to achieve the same productivity as anyone else in a work environment where no one group has an advantage over the other, and to guarantee opportunity for minorities and women based on competence and character and not on circumstances of birth."

Consider, for example, the special gifts and talents of several very different people. They represent diversity in gender, race, and ethnicity. But as I have worked with each of them, I have come to understand that they represent diversity in their different skills, talents, and contributions.

Russ Neal was first introduced to ServiceMaster twenty-five years ago, when he was working in a hospital laundry for the Commonwealth of Pennsylvania. Today Russ is a senior vice president, responsible for the operation of our health care business in the eastern part of the United States, a $200 million business. In his development as a manager and leader, he has used his unique street-smart skills to diffuse tense situations and to negotiate and resolve difficult problems. He says, "I have only two tools: honesty and straightforwardness." Russ has used those tools to develop a special understanding of the people he leads and a close relationship with the customers he serves, and the color of his skin has not been an issue with us.

Bisher Mufti was an immigrant from Jordan when he first heard of ServiceMaster. He spoke only Arabic. That was twenty-seven years ago, and he was working as a housekeeper in West Suburban Hospital in Oak Park, Illinois. Since that time, Bisher has developed as a manager and leader. During the last nine years, he has served as an officer of ServiceMaster and has been responsible for developing our business in the Middle East, Western and Eastern Europe, and Africa. He has a servant's heart and a capacity to do and serve beyond the expected. It is often easy to ignore a non-English-speaking entry-level worker in your company, but I wonder what might have happened if we had ignored Bisher.

When Susan Krause joined ServiceMaster nineteen years ago as an assistant in our legal department, few had the dream, understanding, or appreciation that one day she would be our corporate legal secretary. Soon after the start of her employment, she took the initiative to go to law school, working during the day and going to school at night. Four years later she graduated at the top of her class. She passed the Illinois Bar and assumed a position as staff attorney. As her skills as an attorney developed, she was elected assistant secretary of the firm and then corporate secretary.

Susan was given the opportunity, not because of her gender, but because of her talent, persistence, and vision. Her gifts were developed and nurtured in an environment that accepted her performance and contribution, not one that classified her and tried to advance her just because she was a woman.

Yes, there were times when Susan may have been put down by others because of her gender, all as a result of a bias or prejudice. But such attitudes or actions were not accepted or encouraged as the norm and, when identified, were confronted with the objective of seeking resolution and forgiveness. We all learned in the process, including those who at one time may have thought that women could only do certain jobs.

Wayne Golden was raised in an interracial family, and he started working at a pest control branch when he got out of the navy. After eighteen years with another pest control company, he joined the ServiceMaster family because he saw greater opportunity for growth based on his ability to perform. The proof of Wayne's performance and the confirmation of the opportunity came together when, within five years of coming to ServiceMaster, he was named a division vice president. Like all leaders, Wayne has had to deal with issues of bias and prejudice. He says, "I have found in ServiceMaster an openness to address what is wrong and to seek—and extend—forgiveness, and then to expect changed behavior."

Shinya Tomita is an example of a person who has grown as he has participated in the growth and development of a new business unit. He was one of the first three managers from Duskin, our partner in Japan, to help start our health care business in that market. He quickly learned the basics of the business and brought his important strength of understanding the culture to the development of the business and was able to guide and lead in the adapting of our systems and programs to meet the special needs of this market. Tomita-san has served in every operating position in the business and has been responsible for leading the business to a customer base of over one hundred hospitals. He now serves as a senior administrator of one of the most prestigious hospitals in Tokyo, which was our first customer in Japan.

And the story continues. As I am finishing this book, I have just returned from a trip to China to explore new business opportunities for ServiceMaster. In preparing for the trip, I was briefed on a hospital design project that we had already started in southern China through our Diversified Health Services architectural design group. One of the members of the project team was a young architect named Shu Zhang. Shu was raised and educated in China, and she had come to the United States to get a master's degree. She had only recently joined us and was planning to go back to China for the first time in five years to work on this project and visit her family. She spoke and understood Mandarin and knew the culture. I would have an official translator with me, but she could help me with both the music and the words of what was going on in the various meetings and negotiation sessions. She could also grow in her own development and understanding of ServiceMaster as she had opportunity to participate and understand other areas of our business. So I invited her to join us as part of her trip to China. She was a great help to me, and she grew in the knowledge of our business in the process. As I saw her interact with some of the businessmen and government officials of China, although I did not understand everything she was saying, I knew she was selling and advocating the benefits of our company. She was learning to lead these traditional male Chinese officials who were all senior to her in age and experience to a positive response about ServiceMaster. Her potential was in the process of being unlocked and developed.

As the firm learns to accept God's mix of people, it must be inclusive and supportive, and the boundary lines of exclusion should be few. But there are limitations, and the successful firm also must be selective. The immutables of our firm are as follows:

- Truth cannot be compromised.
- Everyone has a job to do, and no one should benefit at the expense of another.
- We should treat everyone with dignity and worth.
- Our combined efforts are for the benefit of our owners, members, and customers, and not for some select group.
- We must always be willing to serve.

If people cannot agree with these immutables and abide by them, there is no room for them in ServiceMaster. The immutables become standards—or fence posts, if you will—of exclusion, without which a firm such as ServiceMaster could not function with direction and purpose. People who choose not to embrace or implement these values in their work take away from the combined efforts of the firm. This form of diversity is not needed or wanted.

But be careful. As you set a standard of exclusion, remember that *fences* and *fence posts* are not the same thing. What might be a fence of difference is not a wall of exclusion. A few years ago I was meeting with one of our officers, Dave Baseler, as part of the preparation for our annual report. He was concerned that we were not being exclusive enough in some areas of our business, and that we might be compromising or diluting our company objectives, especially our first objective. I suggested that he read the poem "Mending Wall" by Robert Frost, which ends with the aphorism "Good fences make good neighbors." In Frost's New England, stone fences were used to mark property lines. Every six months neighbors needed to "walk the fence," each picking up stones from their own side of the fence and thus "mending the wall." And as they walked, they had the opportunity to communicate and understand each other. The fence was not an impassable wall between neighbors. Instead, it provided a vehicle for common understanding. It did recognize a difference—one neighbor lived to the north and the other to the south. But it was not to act as a barrier to acceptance and cooperation. People who walk the fence line of the firm should be working together—building and rebuilding the wall of their combined effort in serving the customer. In the process, they will communicate, learn, and complement each other and not exclude because of nonessential differences. There are fence posts of exclusion and fences of relationships. The leader of the firm must learn to recognize the difference.

A key to your success in developing the soul of your firm is to harness the power of diversity.

A key to your success in developing the soul of your firm is to harness the power of diversity. Recognize prejudice and be courageous to deal with it when it occurs. Keep the playing field level with your eye on performance. It is a fair test and should be acceptable to all.

As we learn to appreciate the different talents and gifts of those with whom we work, we also grow to understand that we need each other and that differences can bring strength. Thus we need not be intimidated by someone else's uniqueness nor strive to duplicate it. We learn to rely on the overlap of individual differences and strengths, and this overlap builds trust and commitment within the firm. We should encourage independence— but without the malady of autonomy. The firm confronts us with the reality that no one person can do it alone. A diverse and mutually supportive work environment not only makes great commercial sense, it can be fun as we learn from each other.

CHAPTER THREE

Harness the Power of Purpose

PEOPLE WANT TO work for a cause, not just for a living. When there is alignment between the cause of the firm and the cause of its people, move over—because there *will* be extraordinary performance.

**People want to work for a cause,
not just for a living.**

AN EMPTY PROMISE OR A BRIGHT HOPE

SEVERAL YEARS AGO a retired senior officer of one of our competitors visited me. He was complaining about the things that were happening in his former company since it had been taken over by another company. He concluded that too many of the executives and other managers were trying to sell themselves to the highest bidder. They were not committed and were becoming nothing more than hired guns. The mission and purpose of the firm had been lost; it no longer had a cause. Some had been persuaded to stay with added incentives and bonus packages, but where were their hearts? Where was their hope?

His concluding comments to me were right on target. He said, "Bill, you know what makes up a good service company. It's when people feel success in their work and are happy with the people they are working with because they have a common purpose. It's no longer there in brand X."

Samuel Beckett and James Joyce were friends and confidantes. Although the writings of Joyce received more fame and publicity, Beckett won the Nobel Prize for literature in 1969. His essays, short stories, novels, plays, and radio and television scripts are generally obscure and esoteric works stressing the absurdity and despair of life. His characters typically engage in meaningless habits to occupy their time as they wait for a mission or purpose that may or may not give meaning to their lives. When Beckett spoke with unflinching honesty about the emptiness of life without a mission or purpose, he may well have been describing the modern-day worker in an environment of accelerated change and choice, with no hope for the future or mission for his labor.

This is not how things have to be. Every firm should be able to articulate a mission that reaches beyond the task and provides a hope that the efforts and activities of its people are adding up to something significant—so significant, in fact, that even more can be accomplished than is expected.

Why is Shirley, a housekeeper in a 250-bed community hospital, still excited about her work after fifteen years? Shirley has seen some changes. She has been moved from Two West to Three East and actually cleans more rooms today than she did five years ago. The chemicals, mop, and housekeeper's cart have been improved. Nevertheless, the bathrooms and toilets are still the same. The dirt has not changed nor have the unexpected spills of the patients or the arrogance of some physicians. So what motivates Shirley? Does she have a mission in her work? Is she just cleaning floors, or is she part of a team of people that helps sick people get well? Is she ever recognized for what she does? Does she have the best tools to accomplish her task? Does she know that she is needed and is providing an important contribution?

When Shirley sees her task as extending to the patient in the bed and as an integral part of supporting the work of the doctors and nurses, she has a cause—a cause that involves the health and welfare of others. She came to us, no doubt, merely looking for a job, but she brought to us an unlocked potential and desire to accomplish something significant. She recently confirmed the importance of her cause when she told me, "If we don't clean with a quality effort, we can't keep the doctors and nurses in business; we can't accommodate patients. This place would be *closed* if we didn't have housekeeping."

Several years ago our grandson Benjamin was born in England. Judy and I had the privilege of being there with our son and daughter-in-law, Chip and Carey, at the time of his birth. It was a difficult birth, and we were not sure Benjamin would make it. The birth of a baby is always a wonderful miracle of life, but because of the uncertainty of whether Benjamin would live, his birth was an extra-special miracle for us.

A baby is helpless. Everything has to be done for him. All he can do for himself is sleep and eat and sometimes cry. Yet as I looked at this little baby boy who was just seven pounds (or, as they say in England, half a stone) and fit in the cradle of my arm, I realized that all the potential to be somebody was in him. But I also understood that the potential of this little boy would not be fully realized without the investment and care of others.

We all need to be nurtured. In the firm, it is the responsibility of leadership to see that it happens.

We all need to be nurtured. In the firm, it is the responsibility of leadership to see that it happens. The search to be somebody is basic to us all. You may define "being somebody" as achieving a title, position, rank, or even a certain level of income. Others may define it by the size of your house or model of your car. While we never come right out and say it, these types of measurements often become a basis for recognition. But I believe a greater sense of mission and purpose comes when we are given the opportunity to contribute to another by serving, teaching, and helping. We receive as we give, and in the process we understand more of what it means to be somebody. There is great potential for this to occur in our work environment, but only as the leader aligns this potential to serve with the development of the person and the mission of the firm.

A MISSION THAT WORKS

AT SERVICEMASTER WE take our objectives seriously: To honor God in all we do, To help people develop, To pursue excellence, and To grow profitably. These simple statements define our mission and also provide the basis for a continuing dialogue on understanding and applying them in every aspect of our business. That often produces a creative tension between the first two objectives as end goals and the second two as means goals. For example, leaders in ServiceMaster do not have the option of saying, "Today I am going to honor God and not make a profit," or, "Today I am going to make money, and I don't care about developing people." They are continually challenged to make decisions for advancing the firm within the framework of these objectives. If the consequences of a decision or proposed action do not fit, then a change of direction should be taken or no decision should be made.

Our objectives do not ensure a mistake-free environment. But they do provide a constant reminder of the importance of balance.

Some people in our business want to spend more time talking about God than doing their jobs. Others are so busy meeting their bottom-line performance goals that they fail in their training and development of others. We make mistakes. Our objectives do not ensure a mistake-free environment. But they do provide a constant reminder of the importance of balance. A firm that does not develop its people will not be able to care for its customers. A firm that does not profit from its work will not survive. We all make daily decisions in our work that collectively move the firm in one direction or the other. Our objectives provide a checkpoint or early warning signal that helps us understand the direction we are headed.

Providing your employees a cause does not mean that you ignore the monetary side of the equation. A well-designed compensation plan not only provides a way to share results, but allows you to link cause to the reality of where that pay comes from—that is, satisfied customers. For us, this has meant that the leaders of the firm—those who are paid more for what they do and for the responsibility they carry—always have a significant portion of their total compensation at risk. Up to half of their compensation is based on the performance of the unit or business they are leading. A negative variance from budget goals of more than ten percent eliminates the incentive payment. This is a narrow tolerance, but clearly—and I believe more fairly—places the reward with the responsibility. For us, it becomes a way of relating *cause* to *results*.

A clearly-stated mission provides more than a "common cause." It also can provide an ethic for the firm, or way of seeking to do what is right and avoiding what is wrong.

A REASON FOR BEING AND DOING

A CLEARLY-STATED MISSION provides more than a "common cause." It also can provide an ethic for the firm, or way of seeking to do what is right and avoiding what is wrong. The firm needs a moral reference point, a compass heading that provides guidance for the way things are done.

The firm at work operates in a free market system that is morally neutral. The market is indifferent to moral choices. It is blind to good and evil. It is materialistic and impersonal. It is a system that can produce great human misery as well as great blessing. If the firm does not have a moral reference point, it has the potential to contribute to the bankruptcy of the human soul. History has taught us that no organization of people, not even governments, can exercise judgments and decisions in the absence of a moral authority. When they attempt to do so, they eventually revert to coercion, discrimination, and persecution of the powerless. The marketplace and the firms that make it work are no different.

If the firm does not have a moral reference point, it has the potential to contribute to the bankruptcy of the human soul.

Today it is popular to talk about "ethics in business." But the issue is not just ethics in business. It is ethics in life. A discussion about ethics without a reference point reminds me of the comments of E. D. Hirsch in his book *Validity of Interpretation*. He considers the challenge of determining the meaning of words in literature and language and concludes that an attempt to communicate without a reference or standard of interpretation is like going to a picnic where the author brings the words and the readers bring the meaning. We have far too many picnics in the area of ethics, with no controlling standard of right and wrong. The resulting chaos and confusion deprives people of hope and direction in their life and work.

Recently Judy and I spent two weeks in Eastern Europe and Russia. I had the opportunity to work with young business-people from Bulgaria, Hungary, Slovakia, Romania, and Poland who are entrepreneurs in the true sense of the word and who are learning the joys and pains of growing their businesses, selling their products, and developing their markets. I was able to review the progress of our ServiceMaster businesses in the city of

Prague, where in twelve months we had established a beachhead and now are providing management services to seven hospitals with an exciting team of Czech managers. I also spent time lecturing and listening to students in three major universities in Moscow and saw their excitement and desire to learn. But I was frankly depressed with the conditions of runaway inflation, confiscatory taxation, crime, and deceit, which is much of their daily environment. It is as close to anarchy as I want to come, and it is happening in a society that seems void of responsibility or any standard of right and wrong. In response to a question regarding a hope for the future, one student responded with a simple request. He wanted to live in a society where truth and disclosure were more common than lies, deceit, and cover-ups.

Several years ago Alexander Solzhenitsyn gave the commencement address at Harvard University. The title of his address was "A World Split Apart." He concluded that our world is not split over views of the East versus West, or of communism versus capitalism, or of socialism versus the free-market system, but simply over a person's beginning point in determining right and wrong. Is a person to be the measure of all things, or is there a God above the person who provides a source, or reference point, for the straight line of right or wrong decisions?

James Hunter, a sociologist from the University of Virginia, in his recent book on conflicts among people, calls our day a time of cultural wars, where the most fundamental ideas about who we are and how to order our lives individually and together are now at odds. His conclusion is that the nub of the disagreement can be traced to a matter of ultimate moral authority. How are we to determine whether something is good or bad, right or wrong, acceptable or unacceptable? The division or gap in our society, he says, is growing. People living and working in the same community are, in fact, worlds apart.

When you consider that aside from their families people spend more time at work than anywhere else, the firm has a tremendous responsibility—I would call it an obligation—to help people live within a moral framework where some things are clearly right and others clearly wrong. In *The Abolition of Man*, C. S. Lewis wrote that in God's world certain things are right and others are wrong. At ServiceMaster, we have chosen to build our objectives on the conclusion that we live in God's world, and that every individual has been created in God's image with dignity and worth. It is where we begin as we try to determine the *right* way to run our business.

"Okay, Bill," you might challenge, "what makes you think you're right? Why do you start with God? What if I don't believe in God?" These are valid questions. In a pluralistic society, not everyone will agree with our starting point. But few would disagree with the great potential for good as a firm acknowledges that it is right to promote the dignity and worth of every person and the value of serving others. In such an environment, people learn to put the needs of others ahead of their own self-interests or self-gratification.

The worth of every person and the value of serving others provides a reason for our work as we learn to give, not just receive, and to contribute value, not just do a job.

Our first objective is not intended to just express some religious or denominational belief, be it Judaism, Protestantism, or Catholicism; nor is it an attempt to merchandise the free enterprise system or the services we sell wrapped in a religious blanket. We do not use our first objective as a basis for exclusion of people who don't believe in God. It is, instead, the reason for our acceptance of the many differences among people. Because of our starting point, we have a view—a value system if you will—that influences how we seek to operate our business, how we treat our employees, and how we serve our customers. The validity of this ethic should be measured not by what we say, but by what we do.

I will admit that sometimes our first objective causes potential employees to wonder. Tom Scherer is a senior officer who joined the ServiceMaster family in 1986 as part of the Terminix acquisition. At that time he had more than a few questions about our objectives. Were we trying to mix religion with business? As a Catholic, would he be accepted by mostly Protestant leadership? Ten years later he had this to say: "I not only have been accepted, but I have been given expanded opportunities to develop my skills and talents and to live my beliefs. I now realize just how unique it is to be able to work for a company whose objectives align with the personal objectives that Virginia and I had set for our family. They have also helped me to focus on seeking to do what is right in tough business decisions where there are conflicting forces and motives." The worth of every person and the value of serving others provides a reason for our work as we learn to give, not just receive, and to contribute value, not just do a job.

A WAY TO WORK—A WAY OF LIFE

THE SERVICEMASTER ETHIC—OUR WAY of doing business— means that we start with a belief that *people are special*. This fundamental principle affects the firm's dedication to the process of understanding people. It starts with Selection, then Training, then Assessment, and finally, Recognition. We call it our STAR program.

I hope you believe that not *everyone* can work for your company. At ServiceMaster we want someone special, so in our selection procedures we help to identify people who like to serve and care for others. Not everyone can do that. We look for service partners who are strong in what we call "WOO"—Winning Others Over. We often use a profile interview form that we have developed to help identify whether these WOO characteristics are present, because service and caring are part of our objectives. You may need to take a look at your hiring procedures to make sure you are looking for the right people.

In the area of training, you have to do more than just teach people how to use tools or complete assigned tasks. Good training seeks to understand how people feel about their work and about themselves and their contribution to the well-being of those they serve. For example, if you are involved in management, then part of your training should include an experience to see what it is like to do the hands-on work and to feel the emotions of those you are going to manage. That is why we require every manager to spend some time actually doing the task that she ultimately will manage. And it is for that same reason that every employee at ServiceMaster, regardless of position, spends at least one day per year working in the field, providing one of our services to the customer. We call it our "WE SERVE" day. The opportunity to serve a customer is for everybody, including those we recruit into the business as senior officers and those who have been around for a long time.

In fact, one of the reasons Claire Buchan, our vice president for communications, was attracted to ServiceMaster was the fact that, as she put it, "they wanted to treat people well." Her response to her "We Serve" work experience: "Hard! I cleaned Greyhound buses for a day. I spent a long time scrubbing bugs off windshields. I was sore for days! But I gained a new feeling for people who work hard like that every day, and found out how important it is to provide respect and dignity for them as I help to communicate the value of ServiceMaster to the general public."

Regardless of title, position, or responsibility, every leader in ServiceMaster is expected to undergo training and hands-on experience in one or more of our services.

Management guru Tom Peters, who often refers to the importance of building long-term customer relationships, has described ServiceMaster as a firm that seeks to build a "wholesale partnership with the customer." This partnership puts our performance at risk: if we fail to keep a promise, we pay the difference. It is a partnership that seeks to respond to the customer's perceptions and the personality or culture of each organization we serve.

As we partner with the customer, we also partner with the service worker, and our manager must learn to walk a mile in the service worker's shoes. This requirement is an important standard-setter for our firm. Regardless of title, position, or responsibility, every leader in ServiceMaster is expected to undergo training and hands-on experience in one or more of our services.

I joined ServiceMaster almost twenty years ago as a senior vice president, coming to the firm after ten years of practicing law and five years as a college administrator and professor. During the first six weeks of my employment, I spent most of my time in training, learning, and doing the tasks of housekeeping and plant operations and maintenance in several of the hospitals we served, and also learning the basics of carpet and furniture cleaning with local franchisees. To say the least, it was a "different" experience.

As I worked I learned our basic systems and techniques. But the purpose of this training was not for me to become an expert in the seven steps of cleaning a patient room or in stripping and refinishing a hard-surface floor. It was that I could better understand the feelings and emotions, frustrations and joys of service workers as they do what many may describe as mundane tasks. At times I felt like I had lost my identity. A hospital housekeeper is rarely called by his first name. More often than not, housekeepers are addressed with "Hey, you." It was difficult to hear others openly talk about me as if I was not present but was only a part of the furniture or fixtures. However, there were also those special times of joy in being recognized for a job well done or in seeing the response of a patient as a job was done with a smile and pleasant comment.

I have never forgotten the emotions and feelings of serving others and how others may perceive the value of the work being done and the worker. The service worker and our front-line managers are the people on whom the value and reputation of our firm rest. Reputations are fragile. They must be handled with care like a valuable vase that if dropped and broken can never quite be put together again. More often than not, when we fail with a customer, it is because we have not adequately trained, motivated, and understood these front-line people.

Dave Aldridge was one of my recruits and came to Service-Master right out of college fourteen years ago. He, too, understands the importance of knowing how a job is performed and how it "feels." He has worked in both staff and line positions, including leading our people development initiatives at Service-Master. He tells about one of his "We Serve" experiences in a hospital:

"The hospital was opening a new wing, and I was helping to prepare the birthing suites. I was on my hands and knees cleaning baseboards. An excited group of nurses who would be serving in this new area walked through. As they walked by, I looked up and said hello, and no one responded. I wanted to cry out, 'Hey, I have my MBA, and my wife is a nurse!' But the reality was that no one cared or thought I was worth acknowledging.

"The real importance of a 'We Serve' day is not just in the work I do, but in learning what is happening to me as an individual. In my 'We Serve' days, I have learned about the "heart" of our business and about the feelings and emotions of the routine and mundane that are often involved in serving others."

Your view of the person also affects your approach to the development of tools, equipment, and products being used to help people get the job done. If you view people as a costly and unreliable element, then you will look at your machines and technology as a way to reduce or eliminate jobs. We take another view. In the service business, technology provides a *tool* of production, not a *factor* of production. As Drucker has reminded us, this means that the effectiveness of a tool is more dependent on how it is used than on its structure or design. We take that seriously. Our vice president for technical development, Bill

Bond, has developed a "technology" of our standard mop. The texture of the mop handle, the release mechanisms, and the fabric of the mop head have all been designed with both the job and the person in mind. In fulfilling his responsibilities, Bill's empathy for and understanding of people are as important to the success of our research and development function as is his Ph.D.

Our goal is not to find an alternative to people but, instead, to grow people—to train, to equip, and to motivate people to be more effective in their work. A person with both a clear direction and a purpose to serve provides an element of dependability and response greater than any machine. That person is able to meet and solve the unexpected, and to exceed the customer's expectations.

For example, where do you begin when you are faced with starting a $24.4 million contract in a large city school system? Morale is low. More than 14,000 windows are broken in 161 schools. Racial tensions, insecurity among union leaders, and a high rate of absenteeism complicate your task. You have promised a turnaround. The school board members have their necks on the line for hiring an outside contractor, and they want results yesterday!

The answer, of course, is that you begin with people. Kevin Creasman and his team had to make it work. "At the first meeting we had with the employees," he explained, "we provided light refreshments. Everyone came to the meeting and listened to our presentation, but nobody took the food. After the meeting, we discovered why: they did not realize the food was for them. They had never been asked to participate in a meeting where food or service was provided for them."

This was a beginning. We cared for them, and our desire was to treat them with dignity and respect. And soon these same workers responded with enthusiasm in their work and service to others. Within three months of our start date, all 14,000 broken windows were repaired, the air conditioning worked in schools where teachers never knew they had air conditioning, and the appearance of the grounds changed from knee-high grass to neatly trimmed lawns and flowers.

On the anniversary date of our contract, there was an opportunity for assessment and recognition. The city's newspaper ran a front-page story applauding the improvements and quoting school principals who credited ServiceMaster with improving communications within the schools and for organizing the custodial, maintenance, and grounds departments to be more responsive to the needs of administrators and teachers. We had exceeded the customer's expectation in providing a quality service and, at the same time, had saved the school district more than $3 million. And we did it with the same people who had been there before. What happened? The difference began with the way we treated them as people. They already had the dignity and potential. All we needed to do was unlock that potential and provide training, direction, and recognition. It all goes back to our objectives and how we view people.

Even though people work best when they are part of a cause, they still need recognition. Missions can be lonely. And when you are the one who has the mop handle in your hand all day, it may seem a long way from the mop bucket to the ServiceMaster objective to "help people develop." I have learned that it is imperative to provide recognition among peers and with the customer. This becomes an essential ingredient in the motivation process.

Recognition and celebration are often linked at ServiceMaster. Every business unit is encouraged to have an awards or recognition program at least annually, and often the award includes a trip for winners and their spouses to meet together at a resort location for a time of fun and learning.

But you do not have to travel to a resort to recognize the accomplishments of winners. In the hospital or educational facilities we serve, we often sponsor a Pride Day to recognize the importance of the accomplishments of the team working within the facility. Every worker on that team will receive a carnation to wear from the president or administrator of the hospital or school, so that others in the facility will have the opportunity to recognize them for their service. That may seem insignificant to some, but there is value in the recognition process—especially for people who are often ignored. I have seen service workers with tears in their eyes at the end of the short presentation, and they always express their appreciation for being recognized and thanked for the job they are doing. They have been given the opportunity to take pride in what they have done and who they are.

As I have participated in many of these Pride Days, I am reminded of how important it is for a leader to say "thank you." Do you do it enough, especially with those who work closely with you? Have you given them a mission, a cause? Have you walked the front lines to thank them for holding up their end of the deal?

"ServiceMaster brought a level of pride to our schools, and it raised everybody's awareness—custodians' as well as administrators' in the school."

The first time Cassandra Jenkins, a custodian in a county school district, was recognized and thanked for the job she was doing was when ServiceMaster took over management of the custodial department for the district. Listen carefully to the response she gave to a TV reporter who was investigating whether or not ServiceMaster was for real:

ServiceMaster has brought a new level of consciousness to our county, because all of a sudden a custodian isn't just a custodian. She is the person who cleans your school. Custodians are the people who, no matter what happens—if it's raining—if it's cold—they're there at 6:00 A.M. to open that door. And for a long time, teachers or principals might pass by a custodian and not even speak because it was considered to be beneath some people. But Service-Master brought a level of pride to our schools, and it raised everybody's awareness—custodians' as well as administrators' in the school.

Later that same year, in response to a *Wall Street Journal* editorial on family values, one of our managers wrote the following in his letter to the editor:

> Our society has become too secular, too amoral.... Our economic life is probably the most secular facet of our society.
>
> Fortunately, I work for a company that is non-secular and proud of it: ServiceMaster. Reference to God in our company objectives gives us an ethical framework for business behavior....
>
> I can bring my "family values" to work and use them every day. Too few managers are able to do that.

As I listened to Cassandra Jenkins on the *MacNeil-Lehrer News Hour* and read this letter from Jim Horner, who is director of environmental services at one of the hospitals we serve, I realized once again that the process of understanding and applying our objectives was working. People can understand and embrace a cause in their work, a cause that goes beyond just earning a living. The address for our firm—One ServiceMaster Way—is not just a direction to our company headquarters building. It is a reminder to all of us that there can be a way to work and a way to live.

CHAPTER FOUR

The Firm, the Family, and the Promises We Make

SEVERAL YEARS AGO Dick Armstrong had just moved to Denver, Colorado, with his wife, Miriam, and their three children to manage our first company-owned cleaning branch. One day about two months after their move, Dick was sitting at his desk when in walked CEO Ken Hansen—unannounced! Dick scrambled to pull together a review of the business. As the afternoon went on, Dick asked Ken what his plans were for dinner, assuming that the CEO of the company had other reasons for coming to Denver than just to visit the branch. But that was the only purpose of Ken's visit, so Dick invited him over for dinner.

Wisely, Dick called home—with Ken sitting right in his office—and told Miriam to set an extra plate at the table. You can imagine the reaction of a young wife with three kids! But Dick played it cool. "After all, what could I do—the boss was sitting three feet from me."

The conversation continued, with Dick masquerading with some innocuous small talk as Miriam protested on the other end. But it was clear that this was absolutely the worst day to spring such a surprise on Miriam. Dick finally relented. "No, honey—don't go to all that bother. Ken and I will stop for dinner and bring home some dessert." Of course, Ken knew exactly what was going on. So after dinner he bought two big strawberry pies heaped with whipped cream, and that's how they showed up at the door.

The next morning Dick drove Ken to the airport and got a valuable lesson along the way: "Now remember, Dick. Ask your wife *first* before bringing someone home for dinner. Your most important responsibility here is to people, and that starts with your family." With that simple statement, he reminded Dick that, as a leader in a firm that values the individual, he would have the continuing challenge of making his business and his family work together.

The firm of the future may well be required to initiate special activities and functions to support the family as part of its operations.

Healthy families are essential to an ordered society and to effective business firms. In light of what appears to be a growing number of dysfunctional family units, the firm of the future may well be required to initiate special activities and functions to support the family as part of its operation. Whenever you make a decision that affects your workers, you are really making a decision that affects their families too. Promotions, relocations, or changes in a position or assignment are not limited to the work environment; they travel home and have a profound effect on every family member.

This is an important "intangible" when it comes to nurturing the soul of the firm. While it would be unrealistic and ill-advised to let family members dictate the firm's decision-making process, it is equally as foolish to ignore their influence or the effect the firm's decisions will have on family members. Your goal as a leader should be to try to make decisions that will complement both the family of your workers and the firm. One of the easiest ways to do this is simply to involve the family as much as you can. For example, at ServiceMaster, spouses are often included in business meetings, and children are encouraged to visit their parents at work and to participate in stock ownership of our company. It is normal, not the exception, to hear a baby's cry or a young child's shrill voice as we conduct our annual shareholders meeting. Paying attention to the family is not just a "soft" issue of employee relations. It can yield tremendous dividends that are mutually beneficial for both the company and the employees.

Today Dick Armstrong has retired from his position as a senior officer with ServiceMaster, but he is still a part of the company. He now works with his wife, Miriam, who bought a Merry Maids franchise business, and with their son Brent, who owns his own ServiceMaster cleaning franchise, which they operate out of the same office in a Chicago suburb. And their oldest son, Rick, who has been a ServiceMaster distributor in western New York State, is moving back to Illinois to join the family business. In one way or another, all of Dick and Miriam's children survived the six moves in eleven years made during Dick's tenure with the company; and with their own spouses, they are now part of their growing, dynamic business and *our* business.

What has caused this to happen? It never could have been legislated or dictated. It was a process that occurred over a period of years with involvement and mutual commitment between the firm and the family. In Dick Armstrong's case, it was a well-intentioned effort by Dick to involve his family in the life of his company.

For Lon and Linda Oury, family and firm came together through "pillow talk"—those late-night conversations between spouses where one recounts the opportunities and challenges at work, and the other offers counsel and guidance. Lon started with ServiceMaster as a staff attorney, and his wife, Linda, owned and operated a small child care center called GreenTree. When ServiceMaster identified employer-based child care as a possible new service opportunity for the firm, Lon and Linda began talking at home about whether there was a possible fit. They soon developed a proposal for ServiceMaster to purchase GreenTree and for Lon and Linda to work as a team in supporting its future growth.

Would it work? After all, we had a policy that husband and wife could not work in the same unit. We both took a risk, and now, five years later, we have a good business with twenty-six employer-based child care centers and more than 3,300 students in the program.

A firm cannot function to its capacity unless its people can rely upon each other and the covenants and commitments they give to each other and to the customer.

Another value that flows from this way of doing business is the value of *covenants and commitments* as a basis for combined efforts and group action. Plainly said, it is the value of a kept promise. Covenant and commitment are terms that apply to the family, but they are also very much a part of any firm that values people. A firm cannot function to its capacity unless its people can rely on each other and on the covenants and commitments they give to each other and to the customer. Some are formalized in a written agreement, such as an employment contract or a contract providing service. Others, usually more important, are represented by oral promises or statements generating reliance or action by another. People need to keep their word and promises to others, even if it is at their own personal risk and sacrifice.

Dallen and Glennis Peterson started the Merry Maids business out of their Omaha home in early 1980. By 1988 they had grown the business to more than four hundred franchisees providing residential maid service nationwide. Ken Wessner, our former chairman, heard through a mutual friend that Dallen might be interested in selling the business, and that other companies were in hot pursuit. We knew it would be a good fit for Service-Master, and within a few days I had my first meeting with Dallen and Glennis. We soon found that we had much in common, both in our business and personal philosophies. We developed an understanding bond of trust.

A few days later I presented to Dallen and Glennis a one-page proposal to buy the business. We shook hands, and one month later we closed the deal. Dallen describes that month like this: "There were some hitches along the way that could have swung things either way. But Bill and I had made promises to each other, and we were determined that nothing would get in the way of those commitments."

If your firm places a premium on people, the influence and binding characteristics of the covenants and commitments you as a leader make with others go far beyond any legal document. They extend to those groups of people who are relying on you for their future, and it is those groups to whom you are truly bound, without any formal writing, to provide momentum and opportunities for them to develop and grow.

Often the promises we make involve both our customers and our people. When these promises are not fulfilled, there is real pain. I remember the time when Chuck Stair, who is now our vice chairman, and I visited a customer who felt we had broken the promise of service and also the promise of supporting our team members in the account. In their minds, we had let them down—we were not people of our word. Our only response was to admit our error, fall down on our knees, and ask for their forgiveness—not an easy thing to do in the business world. I am thankful for their grace, because they did give us another chance. And as we—two of the leaders of the business—personally got involved in helping to fulfill this promise to the customer, we also confirmed our continuing commitment to our team members. More was involved than saving an account. Being honest with our customer and working to correct a wrong also saved jobs for employees and their families. What could have been a loss turned out to be growth, all because we decided to keep our word. As I said earlier, the decisions you make as a leader do not affect just the bottom line of your company. They affect people—employees and their spouses and children.

IT IS NOT A PERFECT WORLD

OF COURSE, OUR objectives do not mean that everything will be done right. In ServiceMaster we have our warts and moles, and we have made our share of mistakes. We have made both good and bad choices. But because of our standard, we cannot hide our mistakes. The people of the firm will not live as schizophrenics, saying one thing and doing something else. When a mistake occurs it is corrected early, or if it continues, it results in an explosion that demands attention from everyone—including top management.

**Mission and purpose, well understood
and implemented, often provides the
best of internal audit controls.**

Mission and purpose, well understood and implemented, often provides the best of internal audit controls. This point was vividly illustrated to me several years ago when I received an early-morning call from one of our managers in a hospital we served. His boss had been involved in a cover-up of a fictitious payroll scheme. Our manager had been told to keep quiet. But he could not keep quiet because it was wrong. It was not what he or his company stood for. He had to expose it and make sure it was corrected. In his frustration, he called me as the president of ServiceMaster. Because he risked going to the top to correct a wrong, the problem was solved before it got out of control.

As we seek to understand and apply a cause for our work, our desire is not to be known for what we know but for what we do. We must be people of integrity seeking to do that which is right even when no one is looking and staying committed whether the test is adversity or prosperity. Yes, these principles can work even in the marketplace.

CHAPTER FIVE

Why Do People Work, Anyway?

Y OU PROBABLY WON'T be surprised to learn that I read the
Bible. One thing I have discovered is that, from the very
beginning, there was work to be done. The story of creation
describes God as working and resting.

I have also learned that not everyone thinks work is such a
great deal. The writer of Ecclesiastes said, "What does a man get
for all the toil and anxious driving with which he labors under
the sun? All his days are work and pain and grief. Even at night
his mind is not at rest. This, too, is meaningless." I am afraid too
many workers view their jobs in much the same manner.

Is work good or bad?

I am not a theologian, but I think it is significant that the
Bible says so much about work. Work is absolutely necessary
for survival. But those who understand the Bible and work realize that it raises an important question about work: Is it a curse,
the result of sin, or is it a gift that God gives us to help us grow?
How you answer that question may have a lot to do with the
way you view work and workers. And if you are uncomfortable
with thinking about the Bible, the question is only slightly different but just as real: Is work good or bad?

I will spare you the history of how religious people tried to answer that question, but I will refer to two groups who have come to some helpful conclusions about work. First, the Puritans, a much-maligned group who were not nearly as drab and stuffy as they have been characterized. They emphasized the relationship between work and stewardship responsibilities. That is, work had a purpose that went beyond the mere making of money. It was a natural outgrowth of the abilities they had been given. People were encouraged to seek a better way to do their work and be more productive. If they failed in this search or refused and chose the less gainful way, they would not be good stewards of God's gifts. Thus, man could labor to be rich for God but not merely for selfish reasons. Wealth was ethically corrupt only insofar as it was a temptation to idleness or sinful enjoyment of life. It is this "work ethic" made popular by the Puritans that has become commonly known as the "Protestant work ethic."

Second, from the Roman Catholic tradition comes the notion that work is a "calling" in the development and dignity of people, yet also has the potential to be used to perpetuate harm and injustice. This was the subject of the papal encyclical, or special teaching, by Pope John Paul II called *Laborum Exercens*. This treatise reminds us that work is as old as life on earth, and its value is to be found in the person doing the work. People are to be the subject of work, not its object. It is when people are used only as the material means of production or as only the object of work that the injustice of "capitalism" may occur.

Of course, the story of work and its influence on people is not limited to religious sources. Adam Smith, in his treatise *The Wealth of Nations*, recognized the significance of division of labor in making work more productive and the work product of the worker more valuable. His conclusion was that productive labor resulted in the making of something tangible that had value. A menial servant's labor, however, did not increase value because he produced no product. Smith obviously did not envision a modern-day service company like ServiceMaster. Even

Karl Marx recognized the importance of productive work and suggested that the labor of men and the work of their hands distinguished them from what he referred to as "other animals." Marx went on to conclude that it was the surplus of such labor, or what we call profit, that was the subject of exploitation in a capitalist society. He, too, did not envision a company like ServiceMaster, where the producers of the profit also have an opportunity to own it.

I recite these few brief examples of how work has been viewed throughout history because they show us that work is more than just performing tasks. It is part of who we are, or at least who we should be.

But what is the role of work today as we approach the end of the twentieth century? Are the ideas of the past applicable to our modern-day experience? We live in a world of change and choice. The forces of a free-market economy are as pervasive as they have ever been, but the work environment—the very culture of the marketplace—changes almost daily. Work is being restructured and reengineered. Firms are being downsized. We are learning that not only our work must be more productive, but also the information we use in our work must be more productive. The technology of today allows work to be brought to the workers instead of the workers to work. We talk about quality circles and working in teams instead of under supervisors or managers. For some, any place where they can plug in a modem is a place of work. We are not only mixing skills and talents in a work environment, we are also mixing cultures, races, and genders. Some have suggested that we have come to an end of the job—that a specially defined task is no longer relevant because it has outlived its usefulness.

At one time we thought that by the year 2000 everyone would be involved in thirty-hour work weeks. The balance of our time could be spent in rest and leisure. But now that the millennium is upon us, it seems more likely that many of us will be working sixty-hour weeks, and the rest may be unemployed. Are we moving to a post-job world? The job was an idea that emerged in the early nineteenth century to help organize work and make it more productive as labor was divided based on skills and talents, locations, and production requirements. But our world keeps changing, and so does the marketplace. Technology has brought more flexibility and freedom in our work. It may mean that we are heading to a post-job world as jobs were once defined, but not a post-work world. There will always be a demand for the value of the combined efforts of people, which is the work of the firm. As people work together and develop their skills and talents, they can express their creativity and enhance their dignity, all as part of performing and producing service and benefit to others. As I noted earlier, it is within the context of the firm that people produce value—value measured in who they are becoming, value measured in what they are producing, and value measured in the worth of their combined effort.

Instead of decrying the rapid pace of change and its effect on the marketplace, why not embrace it?

What an exciting time to be in business! Instead of decrying the rapid pace of change and its effect on the marketplace, why not embrace it? View the changes that are occurring in our jobs and our work as an opportunity to increase the focus of our work and the product of our effort to satisfy the customer's changing needs. Never define work in a way that limits or restricts the firm's ability to change with the customer. This is an exciting challenge of the future as we celebrate work and seek to improve productivity and produce profits. But in the face of such change, some things must remain. One of these is the need to always focus on your customer.

CHAPTER SIX

Does Your Customer
Have a Face?

THERE IS NO such thing as a firm without customers. In fact, the business of every firm is to create and keep customers. It is hard work and it is also one of the best ways to celebrate work. Customers are not companies, institutions, or governments. Customers are people. In ServiceMaster we do not just sell or serve a hospital, or a large automotive plant, or a household. We sell and serve people—people who want solutions to problems, people who may not yet realize their problems or the variety of solutions available.

**There is no such thing as a firm
without customers.**

In my line of work, we create and keep customers by selling an intangible (a service or expectation of a new service yet to be performed and by its very nature not susceptible to precise specification or quantification). Even though your business may sell a tangible product such as furniture, food, or building materials, you are also selling service. In fact, I predict that the most successful firms of the future will be the ones who are as aggressive in selling their service as they are in selling their product. For customers to buy or continue to buy, they must see your service as a solution to their problem or as a benefit they want. Therefore, you must paint an expectation of results and make tangible the intangible.

Some people have skills of selling and others have skills of operating, but few people have both. The tension between sales (painting the expectation) and operating (fulfilling the expectation) is real and cannot be ignored in the management of the firm. Managing this tension in a way that it becomes a creative force—like the tension forces we use to develop the muscles of our body—can build the muscle and fiber of the firm and its people as they serve and satisfy the customer.

Although some may be better at painting the expectation and others at fulfilling the expectation, every member of the firm should view her job as a continuing selling effort. The work of satisfying the customer is never over. It requires star performance.

A Drucker truism that occurs in every firm is that the distance between the star performance and the average always remains the same. As the selling and performing of a new expectation raises the bar, the average or standard performance for the entire firm moves up. It is the only way to effectively move up the average. One of those star performers with the customer in our firm is Ron Kuykendall. Ron has taught many of us how to develop relationships of trust and confidence with the customer and even how to secure forgiveness when that inevitable mistake occurs. He keeps raising the bar for others to follow because he believes in the potential of people.

That belief comes partly from a time when someone believed in Ron's potential. Ron had finished most of his college course work toward his degree when he came to ServiceMaster but had not taken the final comprehensive exams. One day, when he had been with the company for several years, he got a note from Ken Wessner that read, "Ron, you're so close to a degree. Doesn't it make sense to finish?" Ken helped Ron to arrange with his major professor to do some special work and write a report that enabled him to finish what he had started many years before. "It was Ken's fatherly push," says Ron, "and his interest and love that were the impetus to my finally getting my degree. He taught me how important it is to invest in people to build relationships that go beyond what is required, and to be a friend of those I serve." Ron has gotten out of a sickbed, worked all night, delayed a promotion, and relocated his family from the east coast to the west coast and back again—all as part of serving the customer. He has a big heart—at times maybe too big.

Our penchant for continuous improvement as we serve our customers is represented by our third objective: To pursue excellence. For every service we provide, whether it be managing a custodial and grounds department for a school district or cleaning a carpet for a homeowner, the customer has asked the basic question, "Why shouldn't I do it myself?" We have a business, not because of a patent, a unique product, or a location. We have a business only because we are proving every day to customers that they receive an added benefit by using ServiceMaster. This requires a continual pursuit of excellence on our part and a standard of truth that admits a mistake and calls for the search of a better way to solve any problem.

In our pursuit of excellence, we are often pleased but never satisfied. Soon after I started my employment with Service-Master, Ken Hansen, who was at that time our chairman, taught me a very practical lesson on the value of work and the pursuit of excellence. During the day, I was working in the field learning about how we delivered our services. In the evening, I was trying to keep up with my job as senior vice president. Ken had given me an assignment that required an analysis of certain financial alternatives. It was my first memorandum for Ken, and I worked hard on giving it what I thought was my very best. When the time came to review my work, I noticed that there were many red marks on his copy. He started out the conversation by saying he was *pleased* but not *satisfied*. This statement initially made me mad. But as he took the time to explain his thoughts, I soon became aware that I was learning and saw the opportunity to improve and achieve an even better analysis. He helped both me and my work-product to improve.

Once an expectation has been fulfilled and the customer satisfied, a whole new level of expectations must be painted and fulfilled, or the customer will be lost. "What have you done for me lately?" is not the demand of an unrealistic customer. It is a reality when serving people and should be the battle cry that motivates those who are selling and serving to achieve the next level of performance and customer satisfaction.

A customer's perception of service and value may be subjective, yet it is very real. I will never forget a call I received one day from a ServiceMaster manager to come and help him save a customer. The team had done everything possible to satisfy the customer but to no avail. Since we were to pack our bags and be out of the hospital by the end of the week, I called the CEO of the hospital and set an appointment for the next day.

The next morning, before my appointment, I took a complete tour of the hospital with my eye on quality. Using our QPQ standard (Quality Proficient Quotient), the hospital rated 97 percent. I thought I was prepared for our meeting, but soon after the introductions, I quickly found out that the customer wasn't really interested in our QPQ standard. She judged quality at six o'clock every Monday morning when she took a tour of the hospital (by the way, that is a tough time for us; usual weekend shifts are light and there is heavy visitor traffic during the weekend). She had her own perception of quality, and it was limited to Monday morning. It was that expectation we had to satisfy if we were going to stay in her hospital.

One of the biggest problems a firm has to face is entropy—taking a customer for granted and leaving that customer alone until the relationship dies off or is picked up by the competition.

Unless you build relationships of trust with your customers, listen, learn, and respond to their changing needs, and empower your people to correct mistakes when they occur (not days or weeks later after they have been measured), you will not establish an environment for long-lasting customer relationships.

One of the biggest problems a firm has to face is entropy— taking a customer for granted and leaving that customer alone until the relationship dies off or is picked up by the competition. Everything—including relationships—tends to deteriorate with time unless the new, the improved, the changed, is added. Don't wait for the signals of impending deterioration in customer relationships before you act. In the rush to keep up with changes in your business, it can be easy to forget the customer. It can also be deadly.

Customers are people, not organizations or firms. Let's never forget it!

We want our customers to be our friends. I know that is something of a cliché, but I have observed that in reality most companies that have revenue problems often view the customer as an inconvenience. There is a lesson for all of us in the *Peanuts* cartoon where Linus announces to his cranky sister, Lucy, that he is going to be a doctor. "You, a doctor?" she asks. "How can you be a doctor? You don't love mankind." Linus replied, "I do too love mankind. It's the people I can't stand." Linus, we don't have a choice; we must start with people. Customers are people, not organizations or firms. Let's never forget it!

My predecessor, Ken Wessner, who served with Service-Master for forty years, was a great example of how to grow and build the business by developing relationships with customers far beyond those normally held between a seller and a buyer of services. Ken started our health care business in 1962 and served as chief executive officer of ServiceMaster from 1975 to 1983, during which time the company experienced record growth in revenue and profits. Ken made the customer his friend to the point that many hospital CEOs across the country knew him on a first-name basis. In fact, they acknowledged Ken's accomplishments and confirmed their trust in him as a friend and colleague by inducting him into the Health Care Hall of Fame in March 1993.

Ken learned the importance of customer friendship early in his career. In 1962 Ken was looking for that first customer as he was starting our health care business. After making many sales calls, he finally secured an opportunity to make a full presentation to the board of directors of a Chicago area hospital. After the presentation, he was excused from the room so the board could discuss the proposal. As Ken waited outside for the decision, one of the board members came out of the meeting and asked for a copy of our financial statements. Ken knew he was in trouble. We were still a private company. We had a lot of debt on our balance sheet and needed more capital. Although we had plans to go public to pay back the debt, there was no explanation of that on the balance sheet. He asked if he could go back into the meeting to explain the balance sheet, but the board would not allow a further presentation. And as Ken found out later, several board members, after reviewing the financial statements of ServiceMaster, voiced concern about whether or not we had the financial ability to fulfill the terms of the proposed contract. At this critical moment, another board member, with whom Ken had developed a friendship, stood up and said, "Listen, I don't care what is on that balance sheet. I know Ken Wessner, and when he gives his word, he will do the job!" That is what the power of a friendship can do. Without that meaningful relationship of trust, we would not have made the first sale of what turned out to be a $2 billion management services business providing opportunity to more than 150,000 people.

HOW TO "GROW" CUSTOMERS

THERE ARE THREE questions I like to ask when I am in the field with our area or regional managers who are one or more levels removed from directly serving the customer: "How much time in a week or a month do you spend with the customer?" "What is your customer retention rate?" and "What is your cost of acquiring a new customer as compared to keeping an existing customer?" Unfortunately, in most firms, including our own, line managers sometimes lose focus of these important indicators of the health of their business.

Unless the day-to-day implementation of these objectives adds up to more and more customers being served, the market has not placed a value on our purpose and mission.

To help the people of our firm become more sensitive to these vital signs of life, we developed an easily-understood growth goal for our SMIXX-III planning period ending in 1995. We called it "2×5"—to double our customer base in every business unit over a five-year period. This goal also reminded each of us that, on average, it costs five times as much to sell a new customer as it does to keep an existing customer. The ultimate litmus test of the market is the answer to this question:

> At the end of each day, when you add up all of the work of our people and measure the results, are there more or less customers served?

It is also a good measure for the effectiveness and relevance of our four company objectives. Unless the day-to-day implementation of these objectives adds up to more and more customers being served, the market has not placed a value on our purpose and mission. The customer must initially and then continually experience value, or our objectives are just a philosophy or a plaque that hangs on the wall. The vitality of our objectives is being tested and proved in an environment that thrives on results. This is the grand experiment of ServiceMaster.

CHAPTER SEVEN

Productivity as a Virtue

Peter Drucker has defined what we do in ServiceMaster this way: "You provide dignity and profit through improved productivity." Our work is never over, and as people work, they can learn to do more with less and, in the process, achieve dignity and generate profit. Our ability to meet and exceed our customers' expectations is dependent on continuous productivity improvement. The value added for the customer is *more for less*. This benefit, plus a profit for ServiceMaster, is only possible if people are more productive. It is a never-ending quest of defining the task, improving the task, and setting a standard for quality performance, all of which are part of the productivity cycle.

"You provide dignity and profit through improved productivity."

In reaching for a new level of performance, no one should underestimate the significance or importance of the partnership relationship between the manager and the worker. This is an essential element of the productivity cycle. The manager must assure that the worker's task is defined and understood. She must know the skills and talents of those she leads. But the manager must be concerned not only with what the worker is doing, but also with what the worker is thinking and feeling. The worker's sense of self-worth and accomplishment is an important, albeit intangible, ingredient in the productivity cycle. The manager must believe and put into practice the truth that every person has value and worth, regardless of the task assigned or title given. As this occurs, the manager and the workers become partners and form the basis of a team effort. The combined contribution of the team becomes more important than the role of any individual. The manager often assumes the role of coach and advocate, and this role can extend beyond what occurs in the work environment.

Any task, properly defined, can contribute to the dignity of the person.

Pat Asp has grown up in our food service business and has provided a role model of extended involvement with the people she leads. She often refers to her role as the responsibility of caring for the "twenty-four-hour person." Pat started her career managing hospital food service departments, and she knows what it means to work with people who come from less-than-ideal home environments and limited formal education. She recalls a day when she noticed a woman in her department who was limping. She asked the worker about it and found that there was no apparent reason for the problem. So Pat encouraged her to see a doctor to find out what was wrong. A week later Pat saw her again, and the leg had doubled in size. Although managers were not supposed to "interfere" in the lives of their employees, Pat said to her, "You can file a grievance against me if you wish, but you and I are going to the doctor right now." It turned out that there was a carcinoma on the leg, and the doctor said the leg had to be amputated. "Even then, I had to intervene," recounted Pat. "We got a second opinion, and the employee was able to go through chemotherapy and save her leg." Pat learned through that experience that managers must be an advocate for their team members and not give up on them. As you care for your people beyond what they do, they learn to trust you as a leader. They also develop a loyalty to the firm, and they produce.

If the worker understands the task *and* how it fits within the mission and purpose of the firm, he also can be expected to respond in a positive way to the unexpected.

Any task, properly defined, can contribute to the dignity of the person. It makes no difference how routine or mundane the task may seem. The motions of the task are important, but so are the motivation, attitude, and demeanor of the worker. While we at ServiceMaster have a seven-step process to clean a hospital room in a time frame of two-and-one-half productivity units (down from three units several years ago), a smile and a kind word at the right time may be more important to achieving the ultimate result—patient care. As you define the task to include people values and benefits, the worker can achieve added dignity and significance in performance. Without this sense of dignity, the worker will be caught up in the specifics of the task and will not provide the creativity and motivation for improvement. There will be no "productive" result from the partnership between the manager and the worker, because the task will be so boring that neither will have an interest in improvement. The worker, properly motivated by management, knows best how to define and improve the task and how to increase productivity and improve quality. The manager's challenge is to so motivate the worker that the two will work together for this desired result. If the worker understands the task *and* how it fits within the mission and purpose of the firm, he also can be expected to respond in a positive way to the unexpected. It is this potential that is unique to a person and not possible with a machine. When the unexpected happens, the worker not only meets the standard, but exceeds the expectations of the customer. In solving the unexpected, the worker realizes even more of his potential, worth, and dignity. It is a dimension of productivity that provides the "ah-ha" or fun in work.

In solving the unexpected problem the worker realizes even more of his potential, worth, and dignity.

Improved productivity and quality service go hand in hand. Recently one of our managers, responsible for the grounds crew of a large university we serve, involved the service workers in a review of schedules and procedures as part of an overall quest for quality improvement. Among the innovative ideas was the suggestion that the tractor drivers responsible for mowing the campus lawns did not all have to fill up their tractors with gasoline at the same time each morning. This part of the "task" could be staggered throughout the day. That one change added the availability of nine hours to the schedule, which added time to exceed the expectations of the customer, which improved quality and reduced cost.

I also am reminded of my visit several years ago to one of the hospitals we serve in southeast Florida. As our manager was taking me on a tour of the hospital, we came to one of the patient wings with numerous hard-surface floor areas. The manager explained that the quality of floor surface was still not up to snuff. When I asked him what "snuff" was, he and the service provider who was responsible for the area explained that "snuff" was when you could see not only the reflection of the light in the floor, but also the outline of the light bulb. This was a simple but important standard of quality that could be understood by the service provider, the manager, and the customer.

Both of these experiences taught me once again that those who serve and accomplish the task know more about how to improve the task and satisfy the customer than most supervisors or managers.

Productivity becomes a virtue when the task is defined by a result that develops the person and exceeds the customer's expectation. Many quality or TQM programs have been initiated in non-market-driven environments, where the customer and result desired by the customer is, at best, ill-defined. In a market-driven environment there is only one customer—the person paying the bill. The only acceptable result is a satisfied customer. All other results are irrelevant. In ServiceMaster, we have a program called Kaizen. It is a Japanese term for continuous quality improvement and is based on the following five principles:

1. To pursue excellence requires a commitment to Kaizen.
2. Quality is more than meeting a customer's needs; it is exceeding the customer's expectations.
3. To improve, we must have standards of measurement and understand the reasons for variance, with customer review and input.
4. The process must provide room for change that enables the service provider to contribute and help develop the measurement standards.
5. The ultimate litmus test will be the growth in number of customers served.

One of the everyday realities in providing a quality service is that measurement can never be precise and, more often than not, occurs too late to make a difference. Jim Heskett, Earl Sasser, and Len Schlesinger at the Harvard Business School have done extensive research on various service firms, including Service-Master. Their studies clearly indicate that customer satisfaction is directly related to a quick response in solving problems. Mistakes will happen, but when the service provider is trained, motivated, and enabled to correct the mistake on the spot, the customer usually will view the problem and its resolution as a job well done. We should never let the customer pay for our mistakes. It is this zero-defects mind-set that puts the emphasis where it should be—on the training, motivating, and empowering of the service provider to respond on the spot and adapt to the varying and changing needs of the customer.

The challenge for every firm, especially a service company, is to keep top management close to the boss who is delivering the service and to empower the person who deals directly with the customer.

Unfortunately, in the malaise of meeting detailed standards of quality measurement, firms—especially service firms—may be spending too much time seeking to understand the measurement and the variance, instead of seeking to understand, train, and support the person who delivers the service. In a service company, that person is the boss. A continuing relationship with the customer depends on how that person responds to the expected standard of service as well as to the unexpected requests of the customer. The challenge for every firm, especially a service company, is to keep top management close to the boss who is delivering the service and to empower the person who deals directly with the customer to do what it takes to meet or exceed that customer's expectations.

CHAPTER EIGHT

How Structure Can
Strangle the Soul

W HO ARE THE most important people in your firm? Think hard before you answer. Think about titles, status, salaries, bonuses, and everything else that is usually attributed to importance. Then ask yourself again, "Who are the most important people in my firm?"

As far as I am concerned, the most important people in any firm are those closest to the customer. They represent the firm to the customer. They have the greatest influence on whether or not the customer becomes an appreciating asset.

The longer a person is with the customer, the better that person understands what the customer needs and wants, and the better able she is to fulfill those needs and achieve customer satisfaction.

The higher one gets in an organization, the less she knows what the customer needs and wants. So then why do we keep promoting our best-performing people further and further away from the customer? Why do we set an expectation in the firm that success (title, compensation, recognition, and perks) is directly related to the distance and layers of management between the achiever and the customer? And why do we expect and only empower leaders who are far from the customer to be the primary change-makers of the firm?

The failure to recognize and respond to these basic questions is the reason why so many firms lose their life and vitality—and their souls—as they grow in size. Jack Welch, chairman and CEO of General Electric, was recently quoted as saying, "Size is no longer the trump card it once was in today's brutally competitive world. My goal is to get the small company's soul and the small company's speed inside our big company."

Too many large organizations today have been crippled by the cancer of bureaucracy and an expanding midriff of middle management.

Too many large organizations today have been crippled by the cancer of bureaucracy and an expanding midriff of middle management. People are caught up in the activities of the layers but not in results for the customer. They are defending the status quo, preserving a position or a job, maintaining employment, but not initiating or making decisions for change and improvement. This debilitating indifference curve that organizations by their very nature often foster and encourage must be redefined (another way to talk about reengineering) so that the people with the knowledge and information of what the customer needs and wants are enabled and empowered to innovate and improve.

Drucker suggests that the layers of management we put in place to organize and direct the firm are like relay switches. With each set of switches, the firm loses power and response. The challenge for the firm of the future is to continue to press for a flatter organization, not simply to save money, but more importantly to listen to the performers close to the customer.

When it comes to the structure of the firm, we have something to learn from one of the world's oldest organizations, the Roman Catholic Church. There are just two layers of management between the Pope and the parishioner. They are the bishop and the parish priest. The church has long practiced the principle of subsidiarity, the belief that it is a grave injustice to steal a person's ability to make a decision.

STRUCTURE AND SIZE OFTEN GET IN THE WAY

WE ALSO MUST recognize that the systems we have designed for uniformity and consistency sometimes discourage creativity. Our structured organizations, often thought necessary for orderly review and direction, sometimes limit or stifle rapid and flexible response. Our commitment authority standards intended for reasonable control often become bureaucratic and, in some cases, debilitating. A standard governance structure with top-heavy senior management and quarterly reviews by the board of directors can become out of touch and dysfunctional in a fast-changing, entrepreneurial marketplace.

We were far more focused in ServiceMaster when we were small. We did not have the complexity of multiple services and multiple geographical locations that we have today. The people making the decisions and innovations were close to the customer and also had their own money at risk. Thirty years ago the majority of our business involved carpet and furniture cleaning provided through a network of franchisees. Today this segment of our business is less than 5 percent of the total. We doubled our size every three-and-a-half years during this period and added many new services in many different markets and locations. We have grown from a company that was small and insignificant to one that has market dominance and leadership.

Vitality, focus, innovation, and the entrepreneurial spirit tend to naturally deteriorate with each new major increment of growth.

There is strength in this diversity and size. We are far less vulnerable and susceptible to any one market cycle or the economic conditions of any one group or type of customer. We have a level of financial stability today that we did not have when we were small. Our employees have good benefit plans. We have top credit ratings, a strong balance sheet, and a track record of consistent growth in dividends for our shareholders. We no longer ask our senior officers to pledge their personal assets to meet the payroll. But how does one maintain a spirit of innovation in this environment of multiple services with more than 200,000 workers located across the United States and in thirty countries? The law of entropy is at work in our organization as it is in any sizable organization. Vitality, focus, innovation, and the entrepreneurial spirit tend to naturally deteriorate with each new major increment of growth.

In my first year as president of ServiceMaster, I learned an important lesson from my colleagues on the need for the leader to listen and then provide the opportunity for the unexpected. The bulk of our business in 1981 came from providing supportive management services to health care institutions. Growth was beginning to slow in this major segment, and we knew that we needed to develop new services and markets. Our planning process was in place, but we had not yet decided on a change or addition of a strategic new market direction, nor had we completed a review of alternatives with our board of directors.

Rich Williams, one of our managers in Pennsylvania, and his boss, Stew Stambaugh, developed an idea (quite apart from the corporate planning process) to expand our plant operations and cleaning services to school districts, colleges, and universities. Actually, the idea first came from one of our health care customers who also served on a local school board and requested Rich to make a proposal to the school district for ServiceMaster to provide the same type of quality and results that we were providing in his hospital. As these line managers came back to "corporate" with this new idea, they did not receive much encouragement. We were too busy with our own planning, listening to ourselves and not the customer. In fact, these managers were directed by me and others to get back to the job that was before them—to "stick to their knitting," to continue to develop the health care market that we had before us, and to let us at corporate get on with the strategic planning process. The education market was just not our business niche. Profit margins could never be as high as in the health care market because there was not the same need or demand for intensity of service. We thought we had the answers.

Although Rich and Stew dutifully followed our directives, they had grown up in an environment that encouraged them to continue to press their ideas and not give up on the process of selling their bosses on something the customer needed. Their training, their compensation, and their opportunity to participate in the stock ownership of the company all contributed to their willingness to take a risk and press for change.

The next time around, Rich made a proposal that we at corporate could not turn down. He offered to put his entire annual compensation at risk if, at the end of one year, he couldn't sell and start at least four school districts, with all of them running on a profitable basis. He asked for permission to form his own team, separate and distinct from the health care division. He would assume the responsibility of developing the initial training materials to focus on the needs of the education customer, and he wanted my personal support and endorsement.

Stew and Rich not only accomplished their objectives, but opened a market that has become one of our major sources of growth, as we are now serving over 350 colleges, universities, and school districts with an annualized revenue in excess of $400 million.

The key lesson here: Make sure your organizational structure encourages flexibility, change, and innovation.

As this example shows, success in a new venture is dependent on both individual and company commitments. You need champions for a new idea who take ownership in the results and assume personal risk for performance. You must separate the new activity from being crushed by ongoing reporting and performance requirements. You need sponsorship and involvement of top management as well as a clear target for measurable performance and accountability. The key lesson here: Make sure your organizational structure encourages flexibility, change, and innovation.

CHAPTER NINE

People Innovate and Improve as They Participate and Own Results

I F YOU WANT your firm to survive into the next century, you had better be flexible and ready to change. But where is the genesis of innovation? How does a firm grow and keep up with the changing world of its customers?

How does the firm grow and keep up with the changing world of its customers?

Drucker defines innovation as a "change which creates a new dimension of performance." Such change is essential to the life and vitality of the firm. How, then, do you foster, encourage, and empower the people of the firm to initiate change that will create a new dimension of performance?

Empowerment in this context is not the freedom for everybody to do what she wants to do. Nor is innovation the recognition and acceptance of every new idea. Innovation and empowerment go hand in hand. They can be managed. It is both an art and a science, but without measurable performance you will end up with chaos.

In the innovative firm, leaders listen to the ideas of those close to the customer. Since change is a constant, you must continually press for a flat, responsive organization with participation at all levels and ownership in results. Within the firm you must have continuing communication and understanding of the reason for change and the corresponding risk of change without a new level of performance. The people of the firm should celebrate their victories and learn from their mistakes as they innovate and perform.

Innovation and empowerment go hand in hand.

During the last ten years, ServiceMaster has used an aggressive acquisition policy to help foster and initiate change. The people who have come to us through the acquisitions have brought new ideas as they have been given expanded opportunities. There is a long list of examples, starting with Pat Gallagher and Karl Gerstenberger, who came to us with our first major acquisition in 1981. They not only brought with them a great team of professionals in food service to give us an entry into this new market; they also provided needed depth and experience for our senior management team. Later on, Karl also provided leadership and direction in the innovation of a new service for our health care customers that integrated and combined many of the traditional support departments of a hospital into one effective service team.

In 1987 Larry Fenster and his engineering group brought to us the capability of expanding the technology of our service offerings. With his own penchant for preciseness and developing the new, he is now launching a new business opportunity for ServiceMaster called Global Facilities Solutions, which combines more than forty of our separate services to provide one-stop shopping for facilities management.

Jerry Mooney is another example. He came to ServiceMaster in 1993 as part of our acquisition of VHA Long Term Care—a company that manages long-term care facilities. Soon after the acquisition his responsibilities were expanded to include the management of our home health care division. He has helped all of us better understand the opportunities in this growing market of care for the elderly.

For many years, we thought we understood the "health care market." But our understanding was limited to the needs and requirements of the acute care hospital. Jerry and his team provided a new dimension of understanding for the firm and challenged some of our paradigms of the past.

Part of the success of innovation is the good judgment to get out quickly if the idea doesn't work.

But not every idea is a good idea. We have had the painful experience of shutting down innovative ideas that failed. One such idea involved a heavy-duty industrial cleaning process. We had decided to use the franchising method to develop our channels of distribution, and we had organized the business as a separate unit with equity ownership for those who were going to make it happen. We had a champion. We had sponsorship from top management. And we had defined targets for expected results. But we failed. We not only had to bury this mistake but had to take a significant write-off in the process. It is very hard for a successful organization to admit failure, but one should never avoid the discipline necessary to shut something down or to bury the dead. Part of the success of innovation is the good judgment to get out quickly if an idea doesn't work.

THE CUSTOMER PROVIDES THE FOCUS

WHAT MAKES THE difference between recognizing a good idea from a bad one? Empowerment? No. Lack of participation and ownership from those involved? No. Lack of support from top management? No. The best way to tell the difference is to provide an early exposure to the market. When innovation and empowerment are working within the firm, the customer—not the size of the organization nor personal pride—will become the final litmus test.

When innovation and empowerment are working within the firm, the customer—not the size of the organization nor personal pride—will become the final litmus test.

As I say this, I am reminded of a visit I had several years ago with Warren Buffett, who is a noted authority on investments. During our time together, we discussed our various business units, including our expectations of future growth rates. As he often does, he provided some very sage advice in his own special way. He simply said, "Bill, sometimes it's not how hard you row the boat. It's how fast the stream is moving." Innovation in a fast-moving stream and market has a much better opportunity for success than innovation where you must always paddle upstream.

As you innovate and change, there can be no compromise of quality or excellence in service to the customer. You must never be too busy to respond to the customer's request, and you must never implement a system so rigid that it does not serve the customer's wants. Seldom is there justification for calling a customer unreasonable. You must be on a quest for quality and, at the same time, improved productivity. When the members of the firm cannot do both, they will forfeit their opportunity to serve and limit the opportunities for others to develop.

INNOVATION AND RISK OF PERFORMANCE GO HAND IN HAND

As PEOPLE ARE encouraged to participate in the innovative process and leaders actively listen, there is an opportunity to communicate and achieve understanding that with innovation and change comes the shared risk of performance.

What about the future? Is my job secure? Can I depend on a retirement from the company? Will I have another opportunity to be promoted? Can I expect an increase in my earnings? Can I continue to trust the leadership of the firm? What is their commitment to me, to my development, and to my opportunities for the future? These are all valid questions that people ask as they seek to understand their role in the firm.

As part of my continuing listening process among our employees, I often have coffee with various departments or service units. Recently, at the conclusion of one of these coffees, Ron Meeker from our manufacturing division, who had been with us for more than twenty-five years, asked a very direct question: "Bill, just tell me one thing. Is my job secure, and will my stock in ServiceMaster go up or down?" Ron wanted security in his work and in his investment for retirement. The answers to his questions were dependent not only on his performance, but also on the performance of the other people who make up the ServiceMaster family.

The reality of future growth and opportunity in any firm is simply dependent on the performance of the people of the firm. The risk of the future is in their collective hands. At Service-Master we often remind ourselves that growth is not an option. It is a mandate. There must be growth in numbers of customers served and growth in revenue and profits. When growth is not happening, changes must be made. Without momentum, there will be no opportunity or security.

If growth is to sustain itself, the people of the firm must also grow.

But if growth is to sustain itself, the people of the firm must also grow. We must learn to major in people's strengths and not just correct their deficiencies. After all, we hire people for what they can do and not just for what they cannot do. We must reward performance that benefits the customer and doesn't just please the boss. We also must extend rewards to those who mentor and encourage others to develop their gifts. In such an environment, leaders develop, new people take charge, the paradigms of the past are challenged, and change is accepted. The organization is pushed by the thrust of the new developing leadership, and the establishment learns the joy of support and getting out of the way.

One such young leader in our business is Rob Keith. He is a problem solver. Other people gravitate to him, seek his advice, and trust him because they recognize that he wants to help and serve. Title and position have never been that important to him. He works in an unassuming manner and often uses humor to cut through the difficulties of a situation. Rob says, "It's no big deal," when asked what his job is today as head of one of the largest and fastest-growing units in ServiceMaster. He says with a twinkle in his eye, "I come in to work, I call everybody to make sure they came in, I stay until five o'clock, and then I call everybody again to make sure they stayed until five o'clock." Then he gets a little more serious and explains, "My job is to see that the right people are in the right positions, and that they are motivated and have the support and authority to do what we expect them to do, and then to hold them accountable to do it." Rob's leadership provides a force for change that attracts, not alienates. People enjoy working for him because they know he is with them.

Another young leader in our business who is pushing the organization to a new level of performance is Deb O'Connor. As the senior accounting and budget officer of the firm—a job that often brings with it a special level of fear and intimidation— her push is both gentle and firm. Deb is known throughout our organization for her competency, service, and support, as she identifies the results that must be accomplished. At the age of thirty-three, she is leading some very savvy and experienced line officers in reaching a budget goal of more than $4 billion.

The common characteristics in Rob and Deb's leadership are service, support, and initiative. Their bosses don't have to pull them along, nor do they have to be a referee in resolving personnel problems, as both in their own way push the organization and empower their fellow workers.

For empowered individuals to be effective in a common effort, they must also buy into the mission of the firm. Our experience in ServiceMaster confirms the importance of clearly stated objectives. They have become a time-tested standard for us. The past forty years confirm that our objectives work in an imperfect world where there are difficult customers, unreasonable bosses, and workers whose conduct from time to time appears inconsistent with our objectives. In some cases, thorns must be plucked in order for the firm to grow.

The firm can provide the benefit of a supporting and overlapping interdependence where there is help and encouragement when one misses the mark.

No environment is free from mistakes or inconsistencies. Nor can one shield the members of the firm from the consequences of bad choices. But mistakes need not be fatal, nor bad choices a disaster. The firm can provide the benefit of a supporting and overlapping interdependence where there is help and encouragment when one misses the mark.

The job is not the *sine qua non* of life. Interests outside of the firm, such as family, community, and church, should not be subordinated to the mission of the firm. People, however, are increasingly searching for an alignment of their personal values with the values of the firm. And it is the responsibility of the firm's leadership to be proactive in seeking an integration and alignment of these important interests.

But the firm operates in the marketplace where there is one uncompromising standard: you either make money or you don't. If you don't, you won't survive. There are winners and losers. There is a risk of performance, and we all share it together.

The success of innovation and empowerment also depends on the leader's response to failure. A loss does not make someone a loser, and the lack of performance may be the result of out-of-touch leadership. As we developed our Consumer Services business in the mid-1980s, we were confident that lawn care would be a good business for us. But frankly we were not very successful in developing this business. As we had our problems, we also watched what was happening to the two market leaders, ChemLawn and TruGreen. They were also having problems and losing big money for their owners. In the late 1980s and early 1990s, we had the opportunity to acquire both TruGreen and ChemLawn. Could we turn these businesses around? Why were they losing money? During our due-diligence period, we spent most of our time listening to and learning from people in the field. We listened and learned. They had a confidence in what was needed to be done. They were suffering from problems in the organizational structure, marketing and pricing methods, and service initiatives that had been imposed by new management—all with good intentions, but by people who had not grown up in the business and had not spent time listening to the customers and the people serving the customers. There was much confusion at the service level, which provided an opportunity to get back to the basics, identify leadership from within, simplify the job of the service worker, provide support and training, invest in more productive tools, and eliminate unnecessary layers of management.

Don Karnes from TruGreen, a seventeen-year veteran of the lawn care business, was identified by my partner Carlos as the key leader to make it happen. Don and his team have done a great job, and today TruGreen-ChemLawn is one of the largest and most profitable units of our company. Dave Slott, who is part of that leadership team, puts it this way: "The year before we joined ServiceMaster, we lost a lot of money. I don't think anybody expected us to survive. But we knew what was wrong, and we knew how to fix it. To the credit of ServiceMaster leadership, they let us run the business the way we knew how. At the end of the first year in ServiceMaster, we surprised everybody by turning a profit." Sometimes you have to lose before you can win. You will discourage innovation if you pull the plug every time someone makes a mistake.

CHAPTER TEN

Empowerment Comes from Power

EMPOWERED PEOPLE CAN make money and will strive and push for growth. But for empowered people to work together and accomplish the firm's common objective, there must be an acceptance of the legitimacy of power, a framework for authority, and an avenue for participation and ownership of results.

Leadership has to have power in order to empower.

Leadership has to have power in order to empower. Unless leaders earn the right to have the power and it is accepted as legitimate, they will fall into the trap of seeking to implement power through authority and might. To be legitimate, those subject to the power must have the right to participate in setting a standard or framework within which the power is to be exercised. The four objectives of our company provide a continuing framework for our leaders' actions to be tested by the people they lead.

Power in business is suspect, and not without reason. It is, I believe, because management often wields too much power and there is no effective check and balance or governance either at the board level or from that diverse and distant population often referred to as "the shareholders." Unless management first recognizes the need for legitimate power, there can be no effective empowerment within the organization. The practice of servant leadership forces the leader to understand the value of participation and ownership and to be accountable to those being led and to the owners of the firm.

> **Unless management first recognizes the need for legitimate power, there can be no effective empowerment within the organization.**

At ServiceMaster we seek to maintain accountability by requiring our board to be made up of a majority of independent outside directors, by requiring our executives to be at risk with substantial ownership in the company, and by requiring our directors to be actively involved in people development reviews, quality of service to the customer, and protection and care of the environment. We also provide employees the right to appeal arbitrary management decisions.

> **We must as leaders embrace the principle of subsidiarity. It is wrong to steal a person's right or ability to make a decision.**

As we empower people within the firm, we learn to delegate within a framework of authority and accountability, and we should never take back the right to make a decision. We must as leaders embrace the principle of subsidiarity. It is wrong to steal a person's right or ability to make a decision. If we do so, it will ultimately cripple the firm, with people caught up in activities to please their boss rather than to satisfy the customer. Delegation and decision-making at the point close to the customer are imperative.

Delegation without a framework of authority, however, will result in chaos. Three levels of authority must be understood for delegation to be effective: initiating authority, concurring authority, and ultimate approving authority. In a few rare cases, one person may have the responsibility for all three. But initiating authority is found at every level of the firm. For example, one person may have the authority to initiate a compensation increase for another. But that increase may require the concurrence of a superior or the ultimate approval of a senior officer. The concurring and approving process, however, should not be so burdensome as to impede the right to initiate. Nor should the initiator delegate up the responsibility for making the decision that she has the right and power to make.

When a manager comes into your office to ask for help in making a decision, is he seeking counsel or is he putting the problem on your desk? Whenever you allow a manager to put the burden of problem-solving on your desk, he has technically delegated the problem up, and you have assumed the responsibility for doing his job as well as your own. In the process of helping, don't take over the other person's job.

When the firm recognizes and implements these decisions of authority and empowers people to initiate and act, there is a creativity and outflow of energy that encourages innovation.

I remember a day soon after I became president of Service-Master. I had moved into the corner office and had assumed all of the responsibilities typically associated with the office of the chief executive. Ken Wessner, who had previously occupied that office, walked in to see how I was doing, took one look at me, and said, "You look burdened. What's wrong?" I explained to him that I was wrestling with a particular difficult problem, and I will never forget his response. He simply asked, "Why are you worrying about that? Isn't that Ed's problem? It is Ed's job to bring you solutions rather than problems." With those simple questions, Ken reminded me of how delegation should work.

When the firm recognizes and implements these dimensions of authority and empowers people to initiate and act, there is a creativity, an outflow of energy, that encourages innovation—innovation that can be transformed into results.

WHO OWNS THIS PLACE?

MOST PEOPLE THINK that power in a firm comes from ownership. In a sense, that is true. You can buy people's time and their physical presence at a given place. You can even buy a measured number of skilled muscular motions for eight hours a day. But you cannot buy enthusiasm, initiative, or loyalty. You cannot buy devotion of the hearts and minds and souls of people.

People who buy into a result put their "name" over the door as well as the name of the firm.

People who buy into a result put their "name" over the door along with the name of the firm and, as owners of the result, they can provide assurance of consistent and even extraordinary service. Employees with this level of ownership become empowered to improve and achieve a new level of results.

It is important to provide ways for people to make their "ownership" tangible. One obvious way is through ownership of shares in the firm. This has been an important part of the way we do things in ServiceMaster. Today, 20 percent of the stock of our company, valued at over $500 million, is in the hands of employees—the people making it happen. My friend and colleague Dickie Gauthreaux, the president of Terminix, summed it up this way as he spoke to a group of managers about the ownership program he was provided after ServiceMaster acquired Terminix: "We have been doing this kind of business for somebody else all our lives. Now we are doing it for ourselves. We now have the opportunity of seeing the value and results of our labor, and we own what we are producing." Dickie's ownership of results has become a reality. There was a tangible value that could be shared with others, including his family.

Ownership of results does not start with stock ownership. It begins with *dignity*, *pride of accomplishment*, and *recognition for a job well done*.

But ownership of results does not start with stock ownership. It begins with *dignity*, *pride of accomplishment*, and *recognition for a job well done*. Several years ago I was traveling in what was then the Soviet Union. I had been asked to give several talks on the service business and our company objectives. While I was in the city then called Leningrad, now renamed St. Petersburg, I met Olga. She had the job of mopping the lobby floor in a large hotel, which at that time was occupied mostly by people from the West. I took an interest in her and her task. I engaged her in conversation through the help of an interpreter and noted the tools she had to do her work. Olga had been given a T-frame for a mop, a filthy rag, and a bucket of dirty water to do her job. She really wasn't cleaning the floor. She was just moving dirt from one section to another. The reality of Olga's task was to do the least amount of motions in the greatest amount of time until the day was over. Olga was not proud of what she was doing. She had no dignity in her work. She was a long way from owning the result.

I knew from our brief conversation that there was a great unlocked potential in Olga. I am sure you could have eaten off the floor in her two-room apartment—but work was something different. No one had taken the time to teach or equip Olga. No one had taken the time to care about her as a person. She was lost in a system that did not care. Work was just a job that had to be done. She was the object of work, not the subject.

I contrast the time spent with Olga with an experience I had just a few days later while visiting a hospital we serve in London, England. As I was introduced to one of the housekeepers, Nisha, as the chairman of ServiceMaster, she put her arms around me, gave me a big hug, and thanked me for the training and tools she had received to do her job. She then showed me all that she had accomplished in cleaning patients' rooms, providing a detailed before-and-after ServiceMaster description. She was proud of her work. She had bought into the result because someone had cared enough to show her the way and recognize her when the task was done. She was looking forward to the next accomplishment, and she was thankful. You would have thought she owned the company.

What was the difference between these two people? Yes, one was born in Moscow and the other in New Delhi, and their race, language, and nationalities were different. But their basic tasks were the same. They both had to work for a living. They both had modest and limited financial resources. One was very proud of what she was doing. Her work had affected her view of herself and others. The other was not proud of what she was doing, and she had a limited view of her potential and worth.

The difference has a lot to do with how they were treated and cared for in the work environment. In one case, the mission of the firm involved the development of and recognition of their dignity and worth. In the other case, the objective was to provide activity and call it work.

Issues of quality improvement and productivity require careful listening and implementation of suggestions and ideas from the people doing the work.

People will not own the result unless they have an opportunity to participate and understand the reason for their work. If they see no value in what they are doing, they will have no motivation to improve. Issues of quality improvement and productivity require careful listening and implementation of suggestions and ideas from the people doing the work.

One of the best listening practices of a firm that I am aware of is one shared with me by my brother-in-law, Don Soderquist, who is the vice chairman and chief operating officer of Wal-Mart. It is their practice to provide an opportunity at least once a year for all people in the firm to have the right to speak to their boss's boss about anything in the business: about their career, about things that could be improved, or about any employment policies. This fosters the opening up of communication of ideas and concerns on a leapfrog basis. Because there is a regular schedule and expectation for this communication to occur, it reduces the threat to the boss and allows the boss's boss to dip into his business unit and learn in a noncrisis situation. We all need to do more listening to the people of the firm regarding those things that should be stopped, continued, and improved.

Jack Pollock, who leads our Business and Industry Group, has a unique way to dip into the business unit he leads. He calls it "First Monday." Everyone in Jack's group knows that he will be in his office on the first Monday of every month. He calls managers serving the customer, and anyone can call him with a question or a comment. "Most of the calls I get are informational," says Jack, "things like 'I just thought you would like to know that my boss did such and such,' or 'my wife and I are expecting our first child.' Sometimes spouses call to ask how they can help one of our managers with a special problem. But with every call, I take the opportunity to ask what is happening in the account and how we can help them better serve the customer." These calls serve to keep Jack informed but also give employees the opportunity to be heard on any issues that are important to them. They are participating in the decisions and results of the firm. They have ownership.

An important part of pride of ownership comes from recognition of a job well done. Recently a customer shared with me a story about a custodian who cleaned the lobby and hallway in front of his office. Before the arrival of ServiceMaster, the appearance of the area was mediocre at best. Soon after the implementation of the ServiceMaster training programs, the area looked remarkably different. Not only were the floors shiny, but daily attention was given to the details of dusting and furniture location. The custodian who had been responsible for the area both before and after ServiceMaster was asked to explain the difference. His comments were direct. We had not been able to teach him much on the technical side that he didn't already know. The difference was that now his new supervisor had taken an interest in him as a person, listened to him, reviewed suggestions for improvement with him, and then recognized him for a job well done. He now owned the results and was motivated to improve the results.

NO ONE IS PERFECT

ONE OF THE downsides of empowering people to innovate is that you not only get the best from your workers, you can also get the worst. People are not perfect. Some will abuse privilege, steal, lie, or "innovate" only in areas where they will personally benefit at the expense of others. That is the risk of empowerment, but one worth taking. The best way to minimize the imperfections and guide the soul of your firm toward responsible behavior is to never ignore or cover up instances of abuse. People must be encouraged to recognize their failures, correct them, learn from them, and then move on. But, in no event can the firm afford to live with them. In the process, the leader must always remember not to shoot the messenger who brings bad news.

Early in my ServiceMaster career, I was confronted with one of these imperfect situations. As we were preparing to close our books at year-end, I was notified by our chief accounting officer that our outside auditors had discovered a kickback to a customer made by one of our employees. It had occurred in one of our overseas business units that was reporting directly to me.

Although the amount of the payment was not material to our overall results, it was clearly wrong. I was surprised and concerned. As I dug into the circumstances surrounding the payment, my concern grew, because I learned that others in the business unit had known about the payment but did not report it. Not only was it an improper payment, it was also a cover-up. In addition, I discovered that the leader of the unit, although not directly involved, had created a work environment of fear and intimidation. The messengers of bad news were regularly "shot," all as part of packaging a report on good performance for me.

I had failed to dip far enough into the organization to sense this problem. In the process of listening to all the good reports, people had not been encouraged or empowered to be open about the wrongs and the mistakes. We had conditioned people to look the other way and not own a result to the extent of being part of the correction process.

Identifying and resolving the pain of a mistake often tests the durability and vitality of the firm.

Identifying and resolving the pain of a mistake often tests the durability and vitality of the firm. Dr. Paul Brand was for many years a missionary doctor in India working among lepers. His greatest risk was contracting the disease himself and suffering the progressive deadening of his nerves. He had a practice of taking a scalding hot bath once a week. As he felt the pain in all of his extremities, he knew that he had not contracted the dreadful disease. To him, pain meant life. The pain of honestly facing mistakes means life for the firm.

The mistakes I have made as a leader that hurt the most are those that have resulted in breached relationships with others. In seeking to achieve specific performance goals, I have at times pressed too quickly for a result without understanding the subjective factors of fear, insecurity, or risk of failure that were influencing substandard performance. I have learned that people put in a corner must fight or crumble, and the rightness of my position can be lost in the defeat of a person.

Several years ago I had such a painful experience with one of our senior officers. His employment was eventually terminated, and the board supported my decision. The case ended up in court, and there were no real winners. Would it have been different if I had taken more time to understand why the person acted the way he did? It is a question that does not have an answer, but the process of raising it caused me to learn from the experience and to weigh my judgments more carefully in the future.

It is tough work, as any leader knows, to deal with those who refuse to carry their share of the load or to learn from their mistakes. Remember the advice your parents gave you? A rotten apple can spoil the whole barrel. A negative attitude of one person can infect the entire firm. Here is where your leadership can be severely tested. People who are always finding problems with the firm or who think the grass is greener on the other side of the fence should try grazing elsewhere. When they are pampered or accommodated, it is often at the expense of the rest of the firm. You cannot avoid firing some people. If you put up with people who work against the objectives of your company and are not producing, you steal from those who are performing.

LESSONS LEARNED

AS WE HAVE sought to encourage empowerment and innovation at ServiceMaster, we have learned a few things that might help you in your leadership of others:

- The potential for the new always requires testing and piloting. Successful new ideas are rarely developed on the drawing board or by a market analysis or focus study group. In other words, get started. Get your hands in the bucket. Understanding the theory and practical application is important to getting every new venture off the drawing board. Get hands-on experience and start serving the first few customers. Too often ideas are studied and analyzed until they are suffocated.

- Innovators must have elbow room for mistakes but also must be accountable and at risk for the results. No firm can afford innovative bystanders. The involvement of innovating and creating must also carry some risk of failure as well as reward for success. It will not fit the standard compensation patterns of the firm, and unique and different ownership methods will have to be considered and implemented. This has been one of our strong points at ServiceMaster, where we have developed a variety of different ownership plans that not only cover the performance of the company as a whole but also individual units and in some cases individual projects.

- You must have an organizational structure that separates the innovative initiative from the main business and protects the new idea from the crushing big wheel of the firm's operations. New ideas and new businesses just don't start with a regular monthly or quarterly track record. No matter how much thought is given to the business plan, there are always variations that are not on the mark. But the expected results over a period of time must be established at the front end of the venture or idea, or the ship will be rudderless.

- You must have supportive senior leadership that is ready to serve and listen, but also with a discipline to bury the dead. Not every idea will work nor every innovation produce. It is extremely hard for the successful firm to give up a recognized failure and bury an idea, but in Drucker's words, "The corpse doesn't smell any better the longer you keep it around."

The challenge for us as leaders is to provide an environment of innovation, participation, and empowerment.

CHAPTER ELEVEN

Learning Is Everybody's Business

SEVERAL YEARS AGO the ServiceMaster board of directors had a two-day session with Peter Drucker. The purpose of our time was to review how we could be more effective in our planning and governance. Peter started off the seminar with one of his famous questions: "What is your business?" The responses were varied and included the identification of markets we serve, such as our health care, education, and residential; and the services we deliver, such as food service, housekeeping, and maid service.

> **"Your business is simply the training and development of people."**

After about five minutes of listening to the responses regarding our markets and services, Peter told our board something that I have never been able to tell them. He said, "You are all wrong. Your business is simply the training and development of people. You package it all different ways to meet the needs and demands of the customer, but your basic business is people training and motivation. You are delivering services. You can't deliver services without people. You can't deliver quality service to the customer without motivated and trained people."

In a few short sentences, Peter brought home the point we needed to hear. Learning is basic to what we are all about as a service company. And even if your company is not in the service industry, I contend that the opportunity to learn is the best thing you can give to your workers.

But you may ask, "What is the purpose of the firm—to educate or to produce profits? Is the employee a worker or a student? Do we install systems to control and regulate people to act like robots and produce uniform results, or do we look at the variance in performance or even the mistake as an opportunity to learn?"

The modern-day firm must be a learning organization. Learning and innovation go hand in hand.

The modern-day firm must be a learning organization. Learning and innovation go hand in hand. The arrogance of success is to think that what you did yesterday will be sufficient for tomorrow. Leaders must set the pace as both teachers and learners.

The problem for most of us is that we define education by a diploma or a degree or lack thereof. But in reality learning is a lifelong experience. It cannot be limited to a particular teacher, school, or time in our lives. We will never achieve or learn so much that we can rest at the level of our present understanding. We have a lifetime to learn, and it is in our work environment where most of this learning can take place. Learning should be the business of the firm, and the opportunities provided should expand beyond areas directly related to the business.

I never made it as an accountant, and those in the accounting area of our business often have to put up with some of my "different" accounting ideas or questions. But my good friend Ernie Mrozek, our chief financial officer, never seems to grow weary of teaching me, and in the process, we have both learned some new ways to account for a service business. At times I have been frustrated as I have sought to understand the rationale behind certain accounting rules. But I have learned from Ernie as he has consistently applied an even hand in his teaching and management of me and the rules. He has led me as he has served and taught.

Education within the firm is not the function of any one department. If a manager is too busy to teach, he is too busy to work for ServiceMaster. Teaching enhances the process of understanding. To encourage teaching, we must openly reward those who mentor and develop others. As we look for those people who are ready for promotion, we take into account their enthusiasm for teaching. Which of their subordinates have they helped to develop?

The student is not the work product. He is the worker. The student's active participation and ownership in the results is essential.

At the same time, we must be careful not to transfer the responsibility of learning from the student to the teacher. The student is not the work product. He is the worker. The student's active participation and ownership in the results is essential.

This principle is evident even in the teaching methods we use for basic job skill training. JST, as we call it, is primarily used to teach task-oriented work, or "doing," rather than "being." The process is performed one on one to eliminate the group dynamic of the fear of asking "dumb" questions.

The five-step teaching process starts with a supervisor or team leader explaining the task, then performing the task while explaining it further. The leader then asks the student to perform the task while the leader provides coaching. When this step has been mastered, the student must in turn teach the task to the leader and be prepared to teach it to another student. It is in this step that learning is accelerated. And finally, the teacher and the student learn together how to inspect the work, which closes the loop.

WHY DO WE LEARN?

LEARNING IS NOT just another avenue of self enrichment. The ultimate measure of learning should include a reproductive cycle. The student becomes a teacher and then becomes involved in the process of passing it on. This type of learning results in changed behavior that benefits others.

Those who initiate change will have a better opportunity to manage the change that is inevitable.

We live in a world of change. Change often stimulates learning and provides the opportunity for people to adapt and learn. Max De Pree has used the phrase "the gift of change." But people often fear change. They do not accept it as a gift. In this crucible of uncertainty, there is opportunity for positive direction, provided that those of us who lead are also ready to learn in the changing process. Change in a learning environment provides the leader with a strategic intercept point to interject the new and cause those in the firm to rethink their assumptions and better understand each other and their relationships with others. Without change there is no innovation, creativity, or incentive for improvement. Those who initiate change will have a better opportunity to manage the change that is inevitable.

The firm, then, is like a university, and continuous learning is an integral part of its vitality.

A FIRM OR A UNIVERSITY?

MY VISION OF learning as it relates to the firm goes beyond training for a specific task or project. Executives who seek comfort in the experience of past successes and do not flood their lives with reading, listening, teaching, testing, and new experiences are soon arrogant in their own ignorances and are not leading the firm as a learning environment. A long pattern of success often breeds complacency, which undermines vitality and competitiveness of the firm. Accelerated change and diversity of thought and behavior require flexibility and adaptability within a framework of a continuum of learning. To maintain focus and direction, the leader must not only state and live the beliefs and mission of the firm, but must also allow for the testing of such beliefs and mission. She must maintain a competency and relevancy so that she can be an advocate and provide an apologetic for the belief. The firm, then, is like a university, and continuous learning is an integral part of its vitality. Thomas Jefferson's words for the University of Virginia ring true for a firm with a soul: "For here we are not afraid to follow truth wherever it may lead, or to tolerate error so long as reason is left free to combat it."

When people are working for a cause that can be understood within the context of a mission, the firm and the university become one.

Too often the education process orients a student to please the teacher by giving the "right" answers and avoiding mistakes. I can recall several students I knew who learned to "play back" the information they were given just so they could pass a test. But did they really learn anything? This happens frequently in the work environment as well. Awards are often geared toward performing for someone else's approval rather than working to improve the product of the firm or service to the customer. As a firm grows as a learning environment, we must avoid the cycle of just pleasing the boss, and continue to test for understanding and a corresponding result in changed behavior. As this occurs, the teacher and the learner see the value of their efforts as they provide a benefit to others. When people are working for a cause that can be understood within the context of a mission, the firm and the university become one.

THE SEARCH FOR TRUTH

I BELIEVE THAT learning should spring from a quest for truth. We have found that people can learn to accept and apply value systems as they relate to others in their environment. In so doing, they can learn about who they are, where they came from, and who they may or may not become. In the process, I believe we should recognize and confront a basic issue of life: Is there an ultimate source of truth? Is there room for God?

Learning should spring from a quest for truth.

Allan Bloom, in his book *The Closing of the American Mind*, concluded that the average student attending a college or university today has determined that everything is relative and there is no truth. In such an environment, there is no longer a search for truth. In the absence of searching, there can be no real learning, and therefore we are witnessing the gradual closing of the American mind. The acceptance that there can be truth and the continued process of searching for how truth can be understood and applied are at the heart of our training and development program at ServiceMaster.

This is a living principle that allows us to confront life's difficulties and failures with the reassurance that our starting point never changes and provides a reason and hope above it all. It provides a standard of integrity as we teach and learn with a potential to improve what we do and to enhance who we are becoming.

Several years ago I participated in a class with students from the Harvard Business School. As they were reviewing a case study on ServiceMaster, one of the students asked me a question about our first objective. She said, "Mr. Pollard, in a diverse and pluralistic world with people holding many different types of beliefs, your first objective—'To honor God in all we do'—must offend some people. Couldn't you get the same thing done and just eliminate that first objective?"

God is in the workplace as well as in a church or a synagogue.

You know my answer to that question. But at Harvard you just can't say "no"; you have to give a reason. My response to the student was that, if our first objective had no other purpose than for her to ask the question, then it should be there. The issue of whether there is a God is not something that we need to avoid or hide under a rug. People have a choice as to whether they will respond to God, ignore Him, or reject His existence. But no one should seek to hide the possibility of God or fail to examine the result when one begins with God in the learning process. In a pluralistic society, there is room for God and for people who put the value of others ahead of their own self-interests or gratification. God is in the workplace as well as in a church or a synagogue.

LEARNING BY DOING HELPS US TO APPRECIATE THE SPILLS IN THE KITCHEN

LEARNING IS NOT just a process of correcting or repairing deficiencies. We hire and promote people for what they can do, not for what they cannot do. As people learn, we should encourage them to develop their gifts and maximize their strengths. Learning in the work environment should include elbow room for mistakes. In the absence of grace, there will be no reaching for potential.

**Learning in the work environment should
include elbow room for mistakes. In the absence
of grace, there will be no reaching for potential.**

When we remodeled our headquarters building a few years
ago, my colleague Sandy Jett was given the job of making everybody happy and also bringing the new construction in on budget.
It was a challenging and frustrating job. We had developed an
innovative design to accommodate the change we were making in
the way people would work together, and we were also adding
new office technology. The prices we had originally received
from the contractor turned out to be far too conservative.

Sandy was used to delivering what he had promised, and this
time it was not going to happen. We had to go to the board for
authorization to spend more money. Sandy and I had both made
some mistakes and errors in judgment. He needed encouragement and shade with our board of directors. Sandy and I made
the presentation to the board together, and we received the necessary authorization. He later told me that before the board
meeting he was ready to "fire the contractor and jump off a cliff.
But," he continued, "what could have been the lowest point in
my career turned out to be one of the high points because of the
encouragement and support you gave me." What I didn't tell him
was that, if we hadn't gotten the authorization, I was going to
jump off the cliff with him!

**The potential of the new also requires
testing and piloting.**

As we work with people and give them big jobs to do, we
must recognize the tendency we have to remember the bad and
overlook the potential. In examining the potential of individuals,

we must focus on their strengths and not just their mistakes. We cannot be limited by what they may have spilled in the kitchen.

"If a thing is worth doing, it is worth doing poorly to begin with."

The potential of the new also requires testing and piloting. Successful new businesses are never developed on the drawing board or in market analysis or focus study groups. The successful business must be piloted and tested. Ken Hansen, our former chairman, has reminded us that "if a thing is worth doing, it is worth doing poorly to begin with." In other words, get started, get your hands in the bucket, and understand the theory in a practical application. Soon the time will run out, and if the business is still operated poorly, bury it. But it is important for every learning organization to get that new thing off the drawing board, to get hands-on, and to learn from experience. Too often new ideas are studied and analyzed until they are suffocated.

One aspect of our change from a corporation to a partnership form of organization vividly demonstrates this principle. Under corporate form, shareholders received a short tax form (1099) each year showing the amount of taxable dividends. They only had to enter that number in one place on their tax return. But under partnership form, we had to issue a "K1," which can be a very complicated document. The first K1 we sent out in 1987 required two mailings to shareholders, was more than twenty pages long, and necessitated individual taxpayers to make as many as ten different entries on six different forms. We knew that was not acceptable in the long term. Bruce Duncan and his tax team kept working on improving the process. Last year our K1s had only two numbers to be entered on the tax return, and Bruce is still working on getting that to just one entry. Had we waited until we had resolved this issue, we would never have been able to accomplish the major benefit of partnership form for our shareholders—which has been measured by some to be over one billion dollars. Thanks, Bruce, for getting your hands in the bucket.

It is not always what we know or analyze *before* we make a decision that makes it a great decision. It is what we do *after* we make the decision to implement and execute it that makes it a good decision. More than thirty-five years ago Judy and I made a decision to get married. We thought we knew a lot about each other, but we really didn't. We knew we were attracted to each other, but we did not understand what it was going to be like for the two of us to live together and build a family. What has made it a great decision and a great marriage is not what we knew ahead of time, but what we have done since we made the decision.

MORE TO LEARN AND MORE TO ENJOY

ONE OF THE challenges of learning in business is that people want to be entertained. Old methods of teaching just will not work anymore. If you put a group of workers in a room and lecture to them for four hours, they will turn you off and fail to learn.

Education can be fun and stimulating, provided we incorporate entertainment in the learning process and catch the student's attention.

Television has conditioned us to expect a certain degree of entertainment and sensational visual effects as part of the communication process. It has also resulted in shorter attention spans and has encouraged most of us to attempt to do at least two things at once during the listening process. Many times people are not learning because they are bored. But education can be fun and stimulating, provided we incorporate entertainment in the learning process and catch the student's attention.

For today's audiences with shorter attention-spans, videos, CD-ROMs, the computer, interactive compact disks (CDIs), and other technologies can make the transfer of information more powerful and effective. For example, ServiceMaster has recently prepared a series of CDIs containing short discussion clips by leaders of ServiceMaster as they share their views on our company objectives and on our twenty-one principles of leadership. Our size and diversity of locations means that it may be the only way for some of us to touch and communicate with managers in many locations.

Information is a source of learning. But unless it is organized, processed, and available to the right people in a format for decision making, it is a burden, not a benefit.

Information is a source of learning. But unless it is organized, processed, and available to the right people in a format for decision making, it is a burden, not a benefit. It is just data, not information. In some cases, we are still using and designing information to flow upstream so that top management can control the organization. But why can't we look at information as something that should flow the natural way—downstream. Shouldn't it flow down from a common database to help the front-line managers make good decisions? What information do they need to get the job done? This query should be the fundamental inquiry for information planning in the firm. Information flow should be reviewed continually, tracing the decision-making process and the various transactions that support the delivery of the product or service to the customer. Too much of the work of middle managers today is simply to pass information up and down. As we said before, with each relay switch or layer of management, you double the noise and cut the power in half.

**The firm needs people who can think,
make judgments, and be accountable and
responsible for their actions.**

WE LEARN AS WE PARTICIPATE

PEOPLE WANT GREATER participation in decisions that affect their welfare and their future. This is true not only in the work environment, but also in our schools.

Several years ago I had the opportunity to visit one of our education customers. As I was touring a grade-school facility with the principal, a third-grade student came up to her and asked when she could become a member of the student committee that was reviewing teacher performance. What will be her expectation of participation when she joins the work force? Will we be prepared for her? What information will she need? What will motivate her to be excited about a continuing learning process? How will her potential be fully developed? The firm needs people who can think, make judgments, and be accountable and responsible for their actions. The coming generations will want even more to say about their work environment.

Today ServiceMaster serves over six million homeowners. We have some understanding of why our customers buy and continue to buy. But we are always learning and also seeking to learn from the coming generation of buyers. How do we prepare for their buying patterns? Our marketing efforts must become a continuum of learning and listening.

Paul Bert heads up this effort and has developed many of our innovative marketing and sales methods, including our easy access point for all of our Consumer Services—1-800-WE SERVE. He has called our attention to the importance of listening and learning from school children as we try to understand both our present and future customers. They are influencing their parents' decisions and are developing strong views about the home of the future—what they want and what they need. Paul and his team keep us thinking about the future. Not all of their ideas and conclusions will work. As they learn and think a step or a mile ahead of the rest of us in the firm, they must also think and relate to the needs and necessities of the present. It is a challenge for good and fertile minds.

A PARTNERSHIP THAT EXTENDS BEYOND THE FIRM

As THE FIRM recognizes its responsibility for the continuous learning process, it should be involved in supporting and cooperating with other learning organizations. This includes our traditional education system, which is facing several perplexing challenges. Issues such as the dropout rate or the at-risk child and lack of parental support or inadequate resources have the potential to impose unacceptable barriers to lifelong learning. As we increasingly move to an information-based society and a global marketplace, such barriers will create a growing gap between the "haves" and "have nots." It could have an even greater economic implication if it results in a scarcity of qualified labor necessary to maintain a competitive edge in the world market.

The business firm is a customer of the school.

To resolve this growing predicament, those in the marketplace must recognize the need to encourage learning and to develop partnerships between the firm of the school and the firm of the business. The business firm is a customer of the school. It can provide more than tax dollars or contributions. It can provide work and a vehicle to apply what has been learned so that the student can make a valuable contribution to others. Curriculums should not be developed without the firm's active involvement. Together, the school and the business firm must respond to the challenge of providing a continuum of learning that includes dropouts or at-risk children so that they too can have lives of improvement, productivity, and dignity.

Our firm has developed a number of these partnerships. They include financial support for the purchase of computer, scientific, and athletic equipment. But even more important to the students and people of our firm, they include the opportunity for active involvement of our employees in the learning and mentoring process as they tutor and relate to the students. The benefits of such a partnership are mutual and long lasting. For the most part, these programs have been developed by our employees under the leadership of Wally Duzansky and many others and have been recognized for their effectiveness, including being designated as one of President Bush's Thousand Points of Light.

The firm is part of the continuum of learning. For all of us—students, teachers, workers, mentors, servants, and leaders—learning *is* a lifelong experience.

CHAPTER TWELVE

Servant Leadership Makes Good Things Happen

WILL THE LEADER please stand up? Not the president, but the role model. Not the highest paid person in the firm, but the risk-taker. Not the person with the most perks, but the servant. Not the person who promotes himself, but the promoter of others. Not the administrator, but the initiator. Not the taker, but the giver. Not the talker, but the listener. People working together to perform a common objective need and want effective leadership—leadership they can trust—leadership that will nurture the soul.

People working together to perform a common objective need and want effective leadership—leadership they can trust— leadership that will nurture the soul.

THE OPPORTUNITY IS NOW

SEVERAL YEARS AGO I was asked to participate in Peter Drucker's eightieth birthday party. My assignment was to speak about the characteristics of the effective executive of the nineties. My task seemed larger than life, especially in view of the distinguished audience and my respect for the wisdom of my friend and counselor Peter Drucker. My talk centered on the people being led, not the leader, and I was reminded then as I am now that we live in a world of accelerated change and choice. The only thing certain about tomorrow is that it will be different from today. This has resulted in a certain discontinuity and dislocation for many people. Employment is no longer as certain as it once seemed to be. We use words like *downsizing, right-sizing,* and *restructuring* to mask the reality that people lose their jobs for reasons other than performance. To be out of work is a frightful experience. To work and perform and yet be uncertain about when the ax will fall often creates destructive anxieties.

There is great opportunity for positive direction—provided those who have been trained to think will *lead and serve*.

But however you view or label the rapidity of change and choice and the lack of predictability in the events that swirl around us and their effect on life and on the firm, I believe that, in this crucible of uncertainty, there is great opportunity for positive direction—provided those who have been trained to think will *lead and serve*.

THE DEMAND IS REAL

IN ALL OF this uncertainty and change there is a constant—people:

- People who are looking for a mission and purpose in their work
- People who are seeking to understand the *why*, not simply the *how to* of their job
- People who have a growing appetite for more participation and ownership in results
- People who are increasingly looking to the work environment for security and, in some cases, relief from the confusion in their personal lives

- People who are creative, productive, and want to contribute
- People who have been created in God's image with dignity and worth

These same people need to be nurtured and encouraged, motivated, and even educated in their work. These are the people who are looking for leadership.

Never has there been a greater opportunity for the free-market system to work. There should be little doubt in anyone's mind that this system, which has been at the heart of the growth and development of our nation, is the most effective system ever for the production of goods and services and the allocation of resources. This market system provides the opportunity and freedom for people to make a choice and participate in satisfying their needs and wants. It is based on a fundamental truth that people are born to be free. Free people innovate, create, and produce. These are essentials to a growing economy and the creation of jobs.

People born to be free will respond to a clear definition of a task and recognition for a job well done. People will grow in their self-esteem and well-being as they learn to serve and contribute to others. But free people also make mistakes. They can fail or do something wrong. For the combined efforts of people to be of value—to achieve results—there must be effective leadership.

KNOW WHY YOU LEAD

IN SERVICEMASTER, LEADERSHIP begins with our objectives: To honor God in all we do, To help people develop, To pursue excellence, and To grow profitably. Thus, our role and obligation as leaders involves more than what a person does on the job. We must also be involved in what that person is becoming and how the work environment is contributing to the process.

Is she growing as an individual who can contribute not only in the work environment, but also in her home and in the community? Do I as a manager and leader have a positive influence on the growth of this person? Do I understand what this person is feeling about herself and others when she is performing the task? Am I willing to walk a mile in her shoes?

Socrates said that a person should first understand oneself as a means of making contributions to others. "Know thyself" was his advice. Aristotle counseled his followers that "to use one's talents to the utmost, one must have discretion and direction." His advice was to "control thyself." But another great thinker changed history—and the hearts of people—with His unique approach to a meaningful life. "Give thyself" were the words spoken by Jesus. In John 13 we read the story of how Jesus took a towel and a basin of water and washed the disciples' feet. In so doing, He taught His disciples that no leader is greater than the people he leads, and that even the humblest of tasks is worthy for a leader to do.

Does this example fit in today's world, two thousand years later? There certainly is no scarcity of feet to wash, and towels are always available. I suggest that the only limitation, if there is one, involves the ability of each of us as leaders to be on our hands and knees, to compromise our pride, to be involved, and to have compassion for those we serve.

For people to grow and develop within the firm, its leaders and managers must be prepared to serve as part of their leadership. Servant leadership is part of our ethic, and it means that the leaders of our firm should never ask anyone to do anything they are unwilling to do themselves. The leader exists for the benefit of the firm, not the firm for the benefit of the leader. When we lead by serving, we are committed to being an *example* for others to follow, an *initiator* for change and growth, and an *activist* for the future.

AN EXAMPLE FOR OTHERS TO FOLLOW

SERVANT LEADERS BELIEVE in the people they lead and are always ready to be surprised by their potential. This should be true even though the person, as Max De Pree recounts, is so different that he wears a coveted service pin in his ear instead of his lapel.

We should never be too quick to judge potential by appearance or lifestyle. As I discussed in chapter 2, the firm at work is a place where diversity is promoted. It is the leader's responsibility to set the tone—does she live it—does she walk the talk? The servant leader learns to accept people's differences and seeks to provide an environment where different people contribute as part of the whole and strengthen the group.

As leaders act on their belief in people, they listen and learn. They work at making themselves available. Their door is always open. They are out and about, talking and listening to people at all levels of the organization. They should always be willing to do whatever they ask of others. This is a simple yet profound test of the servant leader.

At our headquarters building in Downers Grove, we have designed our executive offices as a reminder of this principle of listening, learning, and serving. Nobody works behind closed doors. Glass is everywhere, confirming our desire to have an open office and open minds. No executive office captures an outside window. The view to the outside is available to all working in the office.

**The leader who serves and believes in
people is also responsible for fair compensation
or distribution of results.**

The leader who serves and believes in people is also responsible for fair compensation or distribution of results. How do you compensate and pay people for what they produce? As I mentioned earlier, the ServiceMaster plan seeks to pay based on performance and promote based on potential. We believe that those responsible for producing profits should share in those profits, and those who produce more should share more. It is an aggressive plan that supports our goal of making and beating budgets, with a low tolerance if we miss our plan. Over the past twenty years, the incentives and profit sharing paid by Service-Master to its people have averaged 45 to 50 percent of incremental growth in earnings. The people producing the results have shared in the results as they have also contributed to the growth of the firm. They have also shared in the ownership of the firm. More than 20 percent of ServiceMaster is now owned by the employees who are making it happen.

The truth of what we say is told by what we do. This standard of truth requires leaders to be role models and to provide an open environment in which their decisions and actions can be examined. It also requires leaders to admit when they are wrong. This in turn encourages an environment where people report on what has occurred or is anticipated, not on what will make them look good or will allow them to avoid confronting a problem. We should always test our decisions and actions with the expectation of full disclosure to those affected by them. Leaders cannot hide from the consequences of their decisions.

Power is never preserved by the arrogance of deception.

Power is never preserved by the arrogance of deception. Chuck Stair is a partner of mine in business and also a close friend. In his more than thirty years with ServiceMaster, he has served in every line position in the company. He is a very open person—so open that sometimes he makes himself vulnerable. But it is this vulnerability that has brought power to his leadership, a leadership that has inspired many to follow.

Chuck set this pace of openness and caring in the early days of our health care business when he was managing a hospital housekeeping department. For example, when employees asked for advice about buying a car, Chuck would not only listen and advise, he would take the time to go with them and help them get the very best deal. People even started asking him to help them figure out their taxes. He was taking care of that "twenty-four-hour person," learning important lessons of leadership that he would use one day when he became responsible for leading a $2 billion business that involved over 150,000 "twenty-four-hour people."

We must be involved in leading people to do things right and to do the right thing.

When we lead by example, we should do so with conviction and purpose. We should think through what is right and what is wrong in executing our responsibilities. We must be involved in leading people to do things right and to do the right thing. But how does one make the right choice? What are the standards, the absolutes, the immutables?

Several years ago I had the responsibility of serving on the selection committee for a new president and chief executive officer of a large public company where I serve on the board of directors. We interviewed some of the top leaders in the industry for this position. I asked each candidate one very simple question: "How do you determine whether something is right or wrong?" The initial response from many was limited to how they determined whether the business was in trouble or not. After I explained that the question went beyond the business issues and involved the question of whether an action was morally right or wrong, the answers were even more confusing. Some concluded that you determine right and wrong by the way you were raised or the views of your parents. Others thought that the reference point was the law. Only a few were ready to identify that their ultimate reference point began with a belief in God or an authority beyond themselves. This experience reflects where many leaders are today. They have not thought much beyond what they are going to do or how to do it. The *whys* of life have not captured their thinking.

Half a belief is no belief at all.

In a competitive market, compromise—that is, accepting half a loaf—is often essential for survival. But compromise of a basic belief, such as truth or seeking to do what is right, does not result in half a loaf. It ends up being half a baby. I am reminded of the decision King Solomon faced when two women appeared before him, each claiming to be the mother of the same baby. His proposal was to cut the baby in half and give half to each woman. This forced the identification of the real mother, because she was willing to release her claim to save her child. Half a baby is no baby at all. Half a belief is no belief at all.

Leadership is no place for a phony.

For my beliefs about what is right to become a reality in the lives of the people with whom I work, I must not only state the beliefs, but also provide an example by my conduct and maintain a continuing expectation and standard for them to follow. The truth of what I say should be told by what I do. Leadership is no place for a phony. It is not a job for someone who can't live without it.

AN INITIATOR FOR CHANGE AND GROWTH

AS LEADERS, OUR job is to make things happen. We are responsible to initiate and, in some cases, create disequilibrium in order to maintain the growth and vitality of the organizations we lead. As I have already noted, organizations by their very nature foster bureaucracy, with people caught up in activities rather than results. People become involved in defending the status quo, preserving position and maintaining employment, but not in making decisions to serve and create value. The leader who makes things happen through others must learn to dip, upset, and redirect these activities of indifference so that there can be continuing effective results to benefit the customer. Leaders should provide elbow room for mistakes but also must insist on accountability for performance. Such a leader learns to initiate what Drucker has referred to as "organized abandonment." It simply means stopping or eliminating activities or functions that are no longer relevant for the future. The leader must always focus on the breadwinners of tomorrow.

The leader must always focus on the breadwinners of tomorrow.

As leaders initiate change, they should be cautious about adding or assigning too many people to a new project. In ServiceMaster we have a saying that we would rather buy a baby grand piano than hire or assign one unnecessary person. At a later date when we may decide we no longer need the piano, we can sell it or chop it up. But we cannot do that with people.

In making things happen through others, servant leaders must always be willing to risk their own involvement for the desired result, including, as Ken Hansen often reminded us, to "move sideways like a crab." Brian Oxley, one of the officers in our business, is a great example of a leader who makes things happen. His units usually meet or exceed budget—not because they have soft budgets or because he is an expert at forecasting. But when things don't happen as planned, he knows how to move sideways like a crab and interject alternatives, with the end result always clearly in mind.

Making things happen requires the leader to encourage and support the entrepreneurial spirit.

I will never forget the time I was with Brian on a Saturday evening in London. I had the idea that we should complete the day by seeing a play at the Savoy. It was *A Man for All Seasons* starring Charlton Heston. As we were leaving the hotel, it became apparent that it was going to be difficult to get a cab to the theater. I suggested to Brian that he go across the street. I gave the bellman a tip to try to get a cab in front of the hotel while I walked up the block trying to flag down a cab from the other direction. After about ten minutes, and now close to curtain time, it seemed like it was going to be an impossible task to get to the theater on time. Then Brian waved, indicating that he had a ride. It was not a cab. Brian concluded long before I did that securing a cab might be the orthodox way to go, but it wasn't going to get us to the theater on time. He was simply hailing down private citizens, asking if they would take the two of us to the theater. On the third try he found a willing party. He got the job done and was willing to take a risk on doing something different to accomplish the task. It is this single-minded focus and commitment to achieve the objective that is necessary if the leader is to serve people. Otherwise, the future will be at risk.

The growth of the firm requires the continued interjection of the new.

Making things happen requires the leader to encourage and support the entrepreneurial spirit. The cost curve never stays in the same place, and the point of maximizing profits while maintaining growth and developing people is always a moving target.

Growth of the firm requires the continued interjection of the new. Without growth the leader will fail in his responsibility for momentum and development of people.

> **You will not win the race by looking over your shoulder. We must learn from the past, not dwell on it.**

A leader is often faced with the tension between short-term targets and long-term goals. The leader must have people preparing for the sprint and others for the marathon. The value of the firm is always measured on future expectations. The past is only a factor to the extent that it indicates future performance. Unfortunately, it is the recording of the past that takes up so much of the time of both the accounting department and the management of the firm. But you will not win the race by looking over your shoulder. We must learn from the past, not dwell on it.

The equation of the marketplace is simple: profit equals revenue minus costs. Without profit the firm will not survive. The markets we serve are like battlefields. No matter how nicely you want to dress it up, we are involved in the war of the marketplace, and every leader should recognize it. There are winners and there are losers. This requires a mental toughness that involves both tactics and strategy. The leader must seek to understand the market, the competition, and the customer's needs while keeping a single-minded focus on performance. For those of us who lead a public company, our standard of performance is measured every day by the price of our stock. One should not bemoan a quarter-by-quarter review and analysis. One should accept it as a reality, a performance measurement, and a challenge to continue to balance the tensions of the short term with the needs and requirements of the long term. In Drucker's words, "a leader must never sacrifice tomorrow on the altar of yesterday."

This penchant for momentum and a vision for the future requires all good leaders to initiate a plan for succession and development of future leaders. This should start with the commitment of every leader not to hang on or seek to retain a position or title, but to always be of the mind that she will serve until a successor is identified and ready—and not one moment longer. It is the availability and readiness of the right person for the future that should determine when a leader steps aside, and not any predetermined date, age, or other artificial criteria. Leaders have their jobs because they can live without them. The position is not there to hold on to.

This penchant for momentum and a vision for the future requires that all good leaders initiate a plan for succession and development of future leaders.

Servant leaders are givers, not takers. Their promise is to serve. It is not dependent on title, position, level of compensation, authority limits, reporting relationships, or who is going to review one's actions. It is not dependent on any perceived importance or lack thereof of the specific task assigned. It is by its nature dependent on health, family situations, and continued acceptable performance. Promises like this do not allow for surprises and do generate reciprocal commitments that will create mutual dependence, not unilateral action. Leaders with such commitment are opportunity seekers, not entitlement takers.

Servant leaders are givers, not takers.

One of the great strengths of ServiceMaster has been the ability of its leadership to plan and prepare for orderly succession. I have had the opportunity to witness and experience the examples of my predecessors, Ken Hansen and Ken Wessner, as they have been role models in preparing, supporting, and getting out of the way.

As I write this book, I am in the process of seeking to follow that example. My partner Carlos Cantu has recently been appointed the fifth chief executive officer of ServiceMaster. Carlos has great operating skills and is a superb team builder. He is the right person for our future. As I worked with Carlos to prepare and support him, he asked for my "expectations" of him as the CEO. The following summary of those expectations may help in understanding how we seek to make succession work at ServiceMaster, overlapping our strengths and weaknesses just like shingles on a roof.

Carlos:

Be your own person. Maximize your strength. Seek help and support in other areas. Be open and vulnerable to those you trust. As you initiate and make change, I have the hope and expectation that you will involve me for advice and counsel. Don't please me or try to keep things on an even keel with the way things were in the past. Do what is right for the future. My expectation is for you to be the most successful and accomplished CEO ServiceMaster has ever had. That expectation now becomes my single-minded goal.

Be an ambassador in both word and deed of our objective to honor God in all we do. You have much to give the organization in understanding the scope of this objective. You will be tested from many directions. Draw few lines. Be patient with those who think they know all of the answers. Remember that we are not a church or denomination. We accept God's mix of people as diverse as He has made or allowed it, yet we stand for what is right. You and I have a faith and trust in Jesus Christ that gives us an inner strength and discernment that not everyone will agree with, understand, or express in the same way. You will have your own way to carry out this objective through the organization. My expectation is that the meaning and purpose of this objective will have greater understanding and effectiveness among the people of ServiceMaster as a result of your leadership.

Be a champion of subsidiarity and growth. How best to organize a firm to both empower and maintain direction will be a continuing challenge. How big should the branches be? How big should the company units be? We know from experience that growth and size are related. The hiving-off process has been one way to manage and set guidelines for organized growth. We also know that there are economies of scale and efficiency of greater size. There is a tension between these two points and it needs to be managed. My expectation is that we keep a bias toward line versus staff, sales versus operations. Keep pushing down decisions. Err on the side of delegation and not centralized control. In my judgment, centralized control will inevitably create a bureaucracy that will stifle the organization. Keep before the firm the importance and example of servant leadership.

Profit growth and profit margin objectives are important. My expectation is that the existing business units should double in profit over the next five-year period. To help assure the result of continued growth into the year 2000, we may need at least one other strong business producer to come on board within the next few years.

Do not waste precious capital on yesterday's heroes.

Be an advocate of ownership. I firmly believe that the person who takes an ownership in the result will be a better performer. In our business it is not the capitalist that produces the wealth, it is the worker. Keep developing ways in which the workers and producers can own a piece of the rock.

Be innovative and sensitive to the benefits of diversity. As you know, this is a big issue in our society. We must recognize that attitudes and mind-sets still must be changed, that performance must always be in the mix, and that visible progress must be apparent to all within the organization and outside of the organization, including our people and our various publics. Perceptions sometimes become realities.

Be jealous with your time, be involved, don't tolerate incompetence. There will be many demands on your time. Don't take on too much outside of ServiceMaster. Keep demanding others to do their jobs. Put the right person in the right job and demand results. Look for those strategic intercept points when you can dip and test the mood of people within the organization and the quality of service being delivered to the customer. My expectation is that you will keep in touch with what is going on in the firm. For you to get the job done, the people around you will have to work as hard and as smart as you do, even a little bit harder. Demand competency, especially in the professional areas. Take time to relax. Take time to pray about the business and the people.

Be planning for the long term. You will lead the long-range planning process for ServiceMaster into the year 2000. It will provide for you a unique opportunity to touch and feel various levels of the organization and to listen to our people and customers. Succession at all levels of the organization should always be on your mind. Keep thinking through and testing alternatives at these key levels. This job will require time spent thinking of the long term—more time than you have ever spent in the past.

Be my partner and friend. My expectation is that we will continue to grow as friends and partners as we work through the transition and I have the opportunity to support your leadership. There can be only one chief executive and you are the person for the job. I am looking forward to working with you and helping the board of directors to be a more effective approver and representative of our shareholders.

Your friend and partner,
Bill

AN ACTIVIST FOR THE FUTURE

THE SERVANT LEADER is not just a bystander, a hired gun, or a holder of a position. He assumes the leadership responsibility for the long term and not just for his own short-term benefit. No enterprise can function to its capacity unless its people can rely on the commitments of their leaders for the future. Leaders must fulfill their "campaign promises."

Leaders must fulfill their "campaign promises."

It is our word and the promises we make to each other that provide the framework for trust and for relationships to grow. Leaders must keep their promises to the people they lead, even if it is at their own personal risk and sacrifice. It is their obligation. One of the best ways I have found to communicate the extent of this obligation is to picture it as a debt—a liability, if you will—on the balance sheet of every leader.

Several years ago I was talking with one of our officers about his promotion to a new leadership position and the opportunity he had to acquire stock ownership in ServiceMaster as part of that promotion. It would mean that he would have to borrow a significant amount of money to purchase the stock. He was delighted about the promotion, but he was concerned about the risk of borrowing money to purchase the stock.

I asked him to make up a simple T account balance sheet so I could review with him his assets and liabilities. The only indebtedness he listed was the mortgage on his house. I then asked him about the indebtedness he had assumed when he took on the responsibility of leading this important unit of ServiceMaster, which involved over one thousand people. How did he list this obligation on his personal balance sheet? How were the opportunities, jobs, and families of these one thousand people going to be affected by his leadership? Would there be more or fewer jobs and opportunities a year from now or two years from now, and would his leadership make the difference? How did he quantify this obligation? It was a responsibility and obligation of leadership as real as any indebtedness he had ever incurred. In fact, it was much larger than what he would have had to borrow to purchase the ServiceMaster stock. And so it is with servant leaders. We have a responsibility and obligation to the people we serve to make a difference. We have an obligation, but we also experience real joy as we see the results of serving and developing others.

A leader who is an activist for the future must anticipate the future by understanding the present. Such a leader must learn to live on the edge by understanding the variance—not focusing on the negative variances, but by learning from the positive variances and understanding the types and antitypes within the firm that can move the average. This variance and incremental thinking keeps the leader at the cutting edge of understanding momentum and direction. The customer retention rate of any business unit is an example of one of those macro measurements at the margin. It is a litmus test of whether the leader is effective in getting the right things done through others in serving and satisfying customers.

The problem with this measurement, however, is that it is always after the fact. How can a leader anticipate the problem and be part of the solution? The answer is in receiving and analyzing regular customer feedback. The difficulty is in organizing and understanding this feedback, as both Bill Dowdy and Breck Swanquist, leaders in different areas of our business, are learning as they initiate new methods of customer feedback. Bill has grown up in our business and brings to this process his experience of serving on the front line, training others to serve, and achieving a record in sales performance. Breck has come to us from the banking industry with a broad experience and sensitivity for the needs and wants of the retail customer. As they both innovate from different perspectives and in different markets, they are learning that the job of listening to the customer is never over, nor should it be.

The information systems of the firm are increasingly important in helping the leader understand the meaning of the variance and implementing decisions close to the customer. Leadership needs to have information flowing upstream. But there should also be a focus on the importance of information flowing downstream, the natural way, to the people who are serving the customer. Too often leaders are caught in a hierarchy of control—using information only to control instead of using it to encourage and guide a firm of implementors and innovators. Collecting customer feedback can help in determining trends and overall improvement or lack thereof. But it can also be very helpful to the front-line manager if it is organized and the information system communicates back to the manager in a way that will help the manager anticipate customer concerns or problems so that they can be avoided.

A commitment to the future often requires leaders to put their own money at risk.

A commitment to the future often requires leaders to put their own money at risk. Servant leaders are not just professional managers. They should believe in "eating their own cooking" as well as "betting their own egg money" on their decisions and the performance of the firm. Several years ago Warren Buffett purchased a significant block of ServiceMaster shares. One of the things that most impressed him about our company was a significant ownership of stock by our senior officers. It was a confirmation to him that we believed in eating our own cooking.

This ownership had been acquired not simply through options that had no downside risk, but through purchase of stock at market and the pledging of the leaders' own personal assets for the benefit of the shareholders.

If you would review the assets of our senior officers today, you would find that we have not only bet the egg money on the performance of the company, we also have most of our eggs in one basket. It is this level of risk and involvement that confirms the leader's commitment to the long haul, a commitment to the people and to the owners of the firm.

As I ask leaders of our firm to make this ownership commitment, I am often reminded of the ownership commitment we ask people to make every day as they purchase our stock in the open market or as they purchase one of our franchises and start a new business. Mike and Jinny Isakson are a couple who put everything they had into buying and building a ServiceMaster business. They bought a ServiceMaster franchise in Bismarck, North Dakota, and as it grew, they added a lawn care franchise and a Merry Maids business. The early days were tough. Mike tells of making an organization chart for his business and putting his name in every block, except for Jinny's name as secretary and controller.

We are all prisoners of our hope. It is our hope that sustains us. It is our vision of what could be that inspires us and those we lead.

As an owner of his own business, Mike understood the importance of an ownership commitment as he was later asked to take responsibility for leading our entire franchise group. His ownership responsibility as a leader now extends to a business that involves more than five thousand franchise owners in the United States and thirteen foreign countries. He knows what they face every day because he has lived it too.

The leader who is willing to serve as an *example* for others to follow, an *initiator* for change and growth, and an *activist* for the future provides hope for those who want meaning in their life and work.

We are all prisoners of our hope. It is our hope that sustains us. It is our vision of what could be that inspires us and those we lead. In implementing the vision, the leader accepts the reality that he doesn't have all the answers. But the result of his leadership will be measured beyond the workplace, and the story will be told in the changed lives of others.

CHAPTER THIRTEEN

Build on the Ordinary and Expect the Extraordinary

So PEOPLE *DO* make a difference. What else is new? Is this just a story of the success of one firm with a unique corporate culture, or can it happen elsewhere?

Build your team of people around the talents and skills of the ordinary person, not just the special skills and talents of those few extraordinary people.

I wrote this book because I think our experiences at Service-Master can be duplicated in other firms. As you seek to implement and apply these principles, one last word of advice: *build on the ordinary and expect the extraordinary*. Build your team of people around the talents and skills of the ordinary person, not just around the special skills and talents of those few extraordinary people. After all, there are many more ordinary people—more to select from; more potential to develop; more opportunity for commitment and loyalty to the common mission of the firm; and more potential to understand, serve, and sell the customer—most of whom, by the way, are also ordinary people.

I am not saying that star performers are not important to the firm. They are, and recognition of them is one of the best ways to improve the overall performance of the group. Yet ordinary people can be trained, motivated, and empowered to achieve extraordinary results on a combined basis.

LOOK FOR THE MARIAS

DON'T WAIT FOR that person with the "right" degree, twenty years of experience, or a track record of successful performance to come along before you get started. Instead, look for the Marias of the firm. Twenty years ago Maria Barany joined the ServiceMaster family as a housekeeper, initially doing what most would describe as menial and mundane cleaning tasks in a long-term care facility we served in the Chicago area. She spoke only Spanish. She had no prior regular work experience and had limited formal education. But she did have the desire to learn and an empathy for others. She wanted to do something significant, and she had hope.

Maria has accomplished much in her ServiceMaster career, not just for herself, but for her teammates and for her customers. She has grown in her responsibility for others as she has developed as a supervisor and as a manager, and she has led the ServiceMaster program in many health care facilities and school districts in Illinois, Wisconsin, and Texas. She is now not only proficient in English, but she has mastered courses at the college level in accounting, history, and English literature. In her career, Maria has accomplished important work objectives as well as important family objectives, including serving and supporting her aging mother. She recently received the highest award granted by ServiceMaster for her management skills and performance. It was an extraordinary performance by an ordinary person. But listen to Maria's own words as she describes what was important to her along the way:

> My friends did all the talking in the initial interview because I did not speak English. It was agony not being able to understand English, and I felt I was missing a lot....

I made a commitment to learn at least one new word a day. I wanted to speak English and be able to talk with my manager. It was marvelous to learn new words every day, practicing new phrases, writing a little bit. My manager gave me encouragement along the way. It soon became my dream to make a career with ServiceMaster, knowing that, in order to be successful, I must be willing to work hard. My plan had three specific points: follow instructions, learn as much as I could about ServiceMaster, and concentrate on refining my English.... Twenty years ago I started as a housekeeper. I couldn't understand English. Today I not only can speak English, but I also appreciate what Max De Pree said: "Leadership is much more an art, a belief, a condition of the heart than a set of things to do." I have had many mentors in ServiceMaster, and they have also known that leadership is a condition of the heart. Their care has benefited me and helped me develop leadership skills and loyalty to the company and its objectives.

I identify with Maria, because without the training, motivation, empowerment, and mentoring from many others, I would not have been able to achieve, perform, and contribute in my career.

Whenever the temptations of title, perks, or position seem to influence me otherwise, I am quickly reminded of the advice I received from a high school counselor. After carefully reviewing my standardized test scores, he encouraged me to seek employment in those areas that would not require a college education. I was one of those ordinary people who, in the opinion of an expert, only had a marginal chance of success at college.

What has made the difference? The test scores were probably an accurate assessment of my deficiencies, but they did not measure desire, attitude, or the possible influence and motivation of others in unlocking my potential.

People have made a difference in my life—people who have cared enough to risk the investment of themselves in me. They have been teachers, mentors, role models, and friends. They have included the people of ServiceMaster, whom this book is all about. But they have also included many others:

- A mother who loved and prayed and was my biggest fan
- A father who gave me a vision for what I could be, even though death took him from me during that critical first year of college
- A father-in-law who, as a busy medical doctor, always took time to listen and support
- A college professor who inspired me to reach beyond college and attend law school
- A woman executive who helped me as a young attorney to overcome a gender bias
- A college president who provided a vision for a change in career and service to others
- A wife who loved, forgave, and always accepted
- Children who grew up to be friends and counselors

Reflection on the important influence of others provides for me a continuing challenge to "go and do likewise."

DON'T BE FRIGHTENED BY THE SIZE OF THE TASK

HAVING HAD THE opportunity to serve in three separate careers—ten years as a practicing lawyer, five years as a faculty member and college administrator, and now almost twenty years with ServiceMaster—I am reminded of the importance in my life of building on the ordinary and expecting the extraordinary. In each of my careers there came a time when I was frightened by the size of the task and felt overwhelmed by my own ordinary limitations and by those around me. Yet the extraordinary occurred.

The first such situation involved a major undertaking while practicing law. I had spent time as a young lawyer working with a large law firm in Chicago learning the ins and outs of the Internal Revenue Code and working on corporate acquisitions. As I grew in my knowledge, I ventured out to form my own law firm and soon found the joys and pains of a growing law practice with responsibility not only for the client's work, but also for recruiting and developing other lawyers, paralegals, and secretarial support.

The ordinary performed the extraordinary, and the deal was closed on time.

Then came the opportunity. A client with a rapidly growing business agreed for it to be acquired by a large public company. The closing had to occur in forty-five days. Many new frontiers had to be crossed, many relationships had to be managed. Halfway through the process it seemed like an overwhelming task. The lawyers on the other side had a Wall Street address. We didn't even have a LaSalle Street address. New tax issues seemed to pop up every day. The staff of our small firm was consumed with this one project, yet we also had to represent our other clients. We were just too ordinary to get the job done. But the team pulled together. The ordinary performed the extraordinary, and the deal was closed on time.

I had a similar experience while working as a senior officer in college administration. Soon after I arrived, the college received notice that it had received a bequest of an interest in an operating coal company. It was during the time of the oil embargo, and the price of coal soon increased from eleven dollars per ton to over a hundred dollars per ton. The value of the college's interest multiplied by a factor of ten, and the complications in the estate seemed also to multiply with the accelerating value of the company. Conflicting interests of family and managers of the coal company resulted in difficult and embroiled legal problems. My job at the college soon involved regular commutes to Pennsylvania and active participation in the operations of the company. In some ways, I had been prepared for this unexpected event because of my law background.

But in no way was I prepared for the scope of the business issues and the judgment necessary to meet the constantly changing and conflicting demands of the various interested parties. I felt very ordinary, faced with an extraordinary task. Nor was the president of the college well prepared for this type of experience, and for that matter, neither were many of the trustees of the school. We were all ordinary people as we sought to resolve and settle the issues before us. But in reaching a solution over a three-year period, we achieved an extraordinary result: a major addition to the college's endowment fund, free of restrictions and legal problems, and without the downside risk of a drop in coal prices—an event, by the way, that occurred soon after we received our funds.

Within three years after I assumed my responsibilities as CEO of ServiceMaster, I found myself in another one of those special situations. After studying the alternative forms of organization for our business and receiving advice from the investment banking firm of Goldman Sachs, we concluded that it was best for our shareholders to convert ServiceMaster from a corporation to a partnership. It would increase our cash distributions to the shareholders and provide additional capital for future growth. A final decision was made on October 1, and the conversion had to be completed before December 31 of the same year to achieve certain tax advantages and avoid certain tax penalties. It meant that our company, which was then approximately $1 billion in revenue, had to be liquidated as a corporation and reestablished as a partnership. We had to secure a review by the Securities and Exchange Commission of our plan of reorganization and shareholder approval. We were limited in time. We were doing something innovative and new, and it all had to occur through the holidays of Thanksgiving and Christmas.

Within weeks of initiating the project, we also were presented with the opportunity to acquire Terminix. This acquisition would provide a major new thrust for the firm in the consumer services market. It was the first big acquisition for ServiceMaster, and it meant that we would have to borrow over

$165 million. It, too, had to be closed by the end of the year. Could we do two things at once?

And then, no sooner had we decided to move forward on both fronts, when we were also presented with the opportunity of acquiring a company that would give us the capability of providing food management services to educational institutions. This acquisition also had to be closed before year-end. Two sets of law firms had to be managed. Many internal accounting and tax issues had to be resolved. The seller of Terminix had others interested in buying the business, so we had to win against competition if we were to be successful in the acquisition.

We had to develop new banking relationships to secure the funding for these acquisitions. Some of our institutional investors were not in favor of the move to partnership form and began selling their stock, and the price of our shares began to drop just as we started sending out proxies for shareholder approval. This added to the task of communicating confidence and calm in troubled waters. In addition to all of this, we still had a business to run and another year to close with growth in earnings.

Once again, it was a time when I felt very ordinary, supported by people committed to accomplishing the extraordinary. Our plan of reorganization and the acquisitions were approved and completed by December 30, with one day to spare.

It was people who made the difference. In addition to Susan Krause, our corporate secretary, who made many personal sacrifices, and Rob Keith, who was then our treasurer and who kept us all on an even keel, there were others whose contribution in managing relationships with accountants, bankers, lawyers, and the investment community enabled us to complete these extraordinary events in record time.

Bob Erickson was our chief financial officer at the time. On the day before Thanksgiving, Bob and others had to get two valuations of ServiceMaster and Terminix, two tax opinions on the two companies as partnerships, and sign-offs on the audits of Terminix for the previous three years. Terminix had had three different auditors during that period, and one of them was deer hunting in the woods of Tennessee that day. Our outside auditors told us that each tax opinion and each valuation would take at least a week to complete. But Bob and the team worked all day and through the night, and by Thanksgiving morning the tax opinions and valuations were completed, and we had received a waiver on the audit sign-offs from the Securities and Exchange Commission.

Bob also assumed another important role in making the reorganization happen. For the partnership form to work for tax purposes, we were advised by our attorneys that we would need to have some individuals act as general partners. This meant that some of us would have to step up and put all of our personal assets at risk for the business. Four of us agreed to do this—Bob, Chuck Stair, Alex Balc, and me. As a lawyer, I knew what I was asking each one of them to do. It was a big risk. But their response was unanimous and immediate. They believed in what we were doing and in me. Not often does a leader have to ask this much. But their response gave me a renewed strength and vitality to accomplish the task.

Vern Squires, who is now our corporate counsel, was another important member of the team. Vern and I had worked at the same law firm when I first graduated from law school, and we had kept in touch through the years. So when the acquisition opportunities were presented, we needed additional outside help quickly. I immediately thought of Vern and called to ask him if he could drop everything and work on these projects. Within hours he was working on the Terminix deal. At one point he and the lawyers representing Terminix worked forty-six hours straight to complete the fine points of the agreement. I later asked Vern to join our senior executive team, and he has made a very valuable contribution to what ServiceMaster is today.

When it was all done, the magnitude of what we had accomplished for everyone in ServiceMaster—employees, managers, investors, and shareholders—came home to me through two simple words of greeting early one morning in January. I had arrived at the office in a hurry to make an appointment. As I was walking briskly through our mail room, something happened that stopped me in my tracks. One of our employee shareholders, Rose Pacholski, called out in a loud voice, "Howdy, partner." That said it all to me. The partnership was in place not only in legal form, but was alive and well in the way we worked. Rose and others had been partners with me in accomplishing an important objective of growth and value.

Making the decision is easy.
Executing is hard work.

As you reach out for the extraordinary, some guideposts may be helpful:

1. Don't wait to react to change. Initiate change so that you will be able to manage the inevitability of change.
2. No one person can make a decision effective. Others must buy into the decision for it to be implemented. Making the decision is easy. Executing is hard work. Every decision has to be sold to be effective.
3. Ordinary people are not smart enough to know everything. Surround yourself with people who can contribute. Don't let the team off of the hook once you have received commitment. Demand results, and do not tolerate mediocrity, incompetence, or a bad apple.
4. If a decision is right for the whole, don't be afraid to give up or risk part of what may be yours to make it happen.
5. Keep your eye on the target and don't be overwhelmed. Take the issues one at a time.
6. Think big. Expand your horizons and let your cup be overflowing.
7. Don't doubt in the dark what you saw in the light.

8. Loyalty is a rare commodity. Nourish it, but don't allow defections to detract.
9. It's the people side of the equation, not the dollar side, that makes a difference. Keep building relationships.

Demand results, and do not tolerate mediocrity, incompetence, or a bad apple.

Maybe the reason we can expect the extraordinary is that, when it comes to people, no one is ordinary. As C. S. Lewis has reminded us, "There are no ordinary people. You have never talked to a mere mortal. Nations, cultures, arts, civilizations—these are mortal, and their life is to ours as the life of a gnat. But it is immortals whom we joke with, work with, marry, snub, and exploit." The potential for the extraordinary is always present.

Maybe the reason we can expect the extraordinary is that when it comes to people no one is ordinary.

SHINGLES ON A ROOF

FOR ALL THESE principles of value to come together and work within your firm, you must learn to build on individual strengths and cover individual weaknesses—like shingles on a roof. We all know what happens to a roof that is not properly shingled. If there is no order to the shingles, major gaps develop. The roof leaks. The same is true in any organization. If the firm has not taken advantage of placing people in areas of their strengths, the potential value of the combined effort is diminished or lost, and leadership has failed. As each person has opportunity to major in their strengths, they also can complement the weaknesses of others. And so the pattern of work can be ordered like overlapping shingles on a roof, bringing strength to the soul of the firm.

As each person has opportunity to major in their strengths, they also can complement the weaknesses of others. And so the pattern of work can be ordered like overlapping shingles on a roof, bringing strength to the soul of the firm.

These same people—each with their own potential for the extraordinary—also have an influence on who you are becoming. *This* is the secret to the ServiceMaster success story. It *is* what our culture is all about. Will it work in your environment and be sustainable? That's up to you.

AFTERWORD

B y the natural process of birth, a son comes after his father. So perhaps it is fitting for a son to say a few words after those of his father. As both ancient and modern stories record, the occasion to speak after a father presents both a challenge and an opportunity for a son: a challenge to respond to his father's accomplishments without bragging or envy and an opportunity to evoke a sense of his enduring character without undue sentimentality or tiresome platitudes. I hope to convey a sense of how the soul of my father's firm, ServiceMaster, has affected the soul of our family.

Many of the people of ServiceMaster know my father as Bill Pollard, former CEO and current chairman of their company, a relentless negotiator, a perpetual generator of ideas, and an intense questioner. While I know this man, I also know a person whom I call "Dad," my Little League coach, my Sunday school teacher, and my three children's "papa." It is from this latter perspective that this afterword is written. I will share from a son's deeply personal and partial perspective my reflections on my father and his work, his friends, his family, and his faith.

I hope to describe my father for you by recalling certain moments when I have seen a gleam of joy in his eye, heard the vitality of life in his voice, and felt the thrill of exhilaration in his touch. For it is through such "moments of being" that the essence of a person bubbles to the surface as a fleeting and fragile record of the shape of his inner character.

As you know from the preceding pages, the "deal" ignites the flicker of his imagination. I still remember a sailboat ride in August of 1986 when he first told me about the "crazy" idea that the investment bankers had about converting ServiceMaster into a public partnership. For thirty minutes he recounted the negatives. Finally I asked him the obvious question: "Why bother?" With a twinkle in his eye, he gripped the wheel of the boat and spoke urgently: "One tax. Our shareholders would only have to pay one tax."

For my father, the tax lawyer turned business executive, this opportunity was equivalent to scaling a famous mountain from a new cliff face. As the tax partner in my former law firm used to say, good tax lawyers know the regulations; great ones can make them dance. The reorganization enabled my father to orchestrate that dance, but for the most part, it was the people at Service-Master whose hard work completed the choreography and whose dedication under pressure gave grace to the performance. As with each acquisition that followed, the deal and the negotiations brought my father great professional satisfaction, but it was the people involved who gave him a profound sense of joy.

The people of ServiceMaster are the second thing that brings joy to my father's heart. Perhaps it is difficult to see the gleam in his eye because of the intensity of his glare, but he cares about the people he works with, not only because they contribute to the firm, but also because they contribute to his life.

I know that my father's single-mindedness—what others might less charitably call his obstinate stubbornness—can be a problem. Like many of his colleagues, I too have spent more than a few sultry afternoons on a sailboat with him vainly looking for a hint of breeze to fill our sails. He almost seems to want to will the wind into blowing. His singleness of purpose can both inspire and overwhelm those around him.

However, I have also had the occasion to sail with him when he did not stop talking about the accomplishments of people at ServiceMaster. He spoke about the young executive whose humor deftly defused a tense situation, or the officer whose intimate understanding of other cultures enabled ServiceMaster to move into new markets. He spoke about the integrity, commitment, and skill of his colleagues. He spoke about his visits with the people directly serving the customer: the ingenuity of a franchise owner building his own business, the challenge facing a hospital manager beginning a new account, and the thrill of a salesperson closing his first sale.

As a family we recognize the indelible imprint of ServiceMaster people on the character of our father. Granted, there were times we wanted to cut the telephone wire after his two-hour "chat" with the office each day of our vacation, or hide the Federal Express box that seemed to meet us at every hotel lobby, or perhaps start a fire with the fifty feet of faxes he received while we were out for an afternoon walk. Yet we know that he is a better man, father, and husband for having worked with the people of ServiceMaster.

In particular, Ken Hansen and Ken Wessner served my father as examples of wisdom, humility, commitment, and grace. As you know from the introduction, Dad had a sort of bumpy interview process when he first applied for a job at ServiceMaster. He did not tell you, however, that one of his final interviews with Wessner and Hansen lasted about three minutes. He was fairly comfortable—one might even say cocky—that he had secured a position, so he decided to press his future bosses for some indication about his potential for promotion. How did he stack up against his contemporaries at the firm? He had pushed too far. Ken Hansen quickly assessed the motive of his questions and curtly responded, "If you are not willing to serve anyone in this company, you are not the right person for this job." Then Hansen quickly stood and walked out of the room with Wessner. Left sitting alone in the office, it was an object lesson that Dad would never forget: to participate at ServiceMaster, he must maintain an intense grip on the interests of others and a light hold on his own ambition.

Dad's family also brings a gleam to his eyes. He loves to see the wonder in his grandchildren's faces as they catch a fish, or pick out candy from the Popcorn Store, or make their annual pilgrimage to Toys-R-Us to select "Grandpa's gift." During a recent Christmas, he arose at five o'clock to put on his Santa suit and surprise the kids. Unfortunately, he fell back asleep on the couch and awoke only after hearing peals of laughter from the older grandchildren as they pulled at his beard and tried to open his bag. Ever since, the few grandchildren who still believe in Santa think that the jolly old man takes a nap at "Papa and Grandma's house" on his annual journey to deliver presents.

Dad also laughs until tears roll down his cheeks at Julie's penetrating humor; he consults with Amy on most of his gifts for Mom; he relishes the opportunity to work with Mark and Brian in their businesses; and he treats our spouses like his own children. He missed growing older with his father, who died when my dad was only eighteen, and he remembers fondly his mother who gave him unwavering support until her recent death. These threads of family relations have been woven into the fabric of his life.

While Dad loves his family, it is his spouse who makes him sparkle with life through the radiant affirmation of her love. Through her gentle, insistent prompting and outright tumultuous battles, she slows him down to see the joys of life that exist outside of work. He, on the other hand, inspires her with new challenges to live out her calling.

In a strange way, my parents' preferred modes of travel best exemplify how they complement each other. For no other person would my dad drive fourteen hundred miles to Florida or take a forty-eight-hour train trip to Washington State. Yet, without Mom, he would not take the time to listen to a great novel as they drive down the interstate or to experience the thrill of seeing the Rocky Mountains from a train window.

Likewise, there are very few good things that my mom can say about airplanes, especially ones that attempt to fly over great bodies of water. Yet, without my Dad's encouragement, she would not have made it to Ecuador to see the water flow for the first time in a Quechua Indian village or to Romania to bring food and Bibles to underground churches. Through this give-and-take, they throw their lives together to form that wonderful arch of human relationships known as marriage.

Finally, there is one more thing that animates my father—singing. While it is difficult to convey this part of his personality in words, perhaps a story will help. Several years ago I made an arrangement to have dinner with Ken Hansen. I wanted to know how we as a family could help Dad as he made the transition from his role as CEO to his position as chairman. I also was facing a career change, and I thought he would be a wise man to consult about my possible options. Finally, I knew that he was not in good health, so I felt a sense of urgency about getting to know this man whom my father so highly esteemed. Following dinner and a lively discussion, Mr. Hansen invited me to join him in his evening devotions, for he was a person who taught not only through word, but through deed. We prayed together and read from the Psalms. And then, to close, he asked me to sing with him from his little Presbyterian hymnbook. With a frantic look of desperation, I furtively glanced around the room, hoping to see a guitar, a cassette deck, or even a pitch pipe that would provide those few vital notes that I needed in order to sing. But this was to be an *a cappella* performance. After struggling through all five verses, he patted my knee, shook his head, smiled, and said, "Just like your father. You sing loud, but not always well."

As I came to write this afterword, I remembered the many Sunday mornings I sat in the green pew at Bethany Chapel and listened to my father sing. It is true. He does sing loud if not always well. But it is because he loses sight of himself in praise to his God. For you see, it is in worship that he becomes most alive. The same intensity that leads to his mistakes, the quick flash of anger, the hasty assumption, or the blunt question also inspires his gifts, his single-mindedness, his loyalty, his concern, his perseverance, his zest for life, his love for God and for others.

So, Dad, keep singing loud and trust God to help you sing well!

—Charles W. Pollard III

APPENDIX

The Twenty-One Principles of Leadership at ServiceMaster

1. We are opportunity seekers, not entitlement takers. We create and earn and cannot afford to sit and inherit.

2. We are value driven and performance oriented.

3. We eat our own cooking. We bet the egg money on our own performance.

4. We train and run for both the sprint and marathon. We rest, have fun, never quit, and always seek to learn.

5. We plan for succession and develop our future leaders.

6. The truth of what we say is told by what we do. "If you don't live it, you don't believe it."

7. If we cannot serve and sell with a passion for excellence, we cannot lead.

8. We believe in what we sell and deliver.

9. As we provide extraordinary service, we bring value-added to the customer that cannot be duplicated.

10. There are no friendly competitors.

11. We believe in a lean and disciplined organization. We would rather buy a grand piano than employ or assign one unnecessary person.

12. We pay based on performance and promote based on potential, not belief, tenure, gender, race, or friendships.

13. Those who produce the profits should share in the profits. Those who produce more should share more.

14. We make and beat budgets.

15. We seek to know and increase our market share so that we can grow and increase the profitability and value of our business. If we ignore our market share, we run the risk of losing our market and our business.

16. When we are wrong or fail, we admit it. Truth cannot be compromised. We report on what has occurred or is anticipated, not on what will make us look good.

17. We promote others, not ourselves. We shoot against par.

18. We must have a spirit of independence without the malady of autonomy.

19. The customer comes first and should be our friend.

20. We are all prisoners of our hope. It is our hope that sustains us, and it is our vision for what could be that inspires us and those we lead. "Don't doubt in the dark what you have seen in the light."

21. We have all been created in God's image, and the results of our leadership will be measured beyond the workplace. The story will be told in the changed lives of people.

INDEX